THE WHOLE POINT OF WRITING SOMETHING DOWN IS THAT YOUR
VOICE WILL THEN CARRY FOR THOUSANDS OF MILES, WHEREAS
IN DIRECT CONVERSATION IT FADES AT A HUNDRED PACES.
– **MATTEO RICCI, S.J.**

Mateus Ricio.

20ARP19

Happy Easter! Hope you
Enjoy this Book from CIB,
when I was in Beijing!

The Beijing Center Publication Series:

Matteo Ricci:
Letters from China

A Revised English Translation with Commentary

Editors:
Brendan Gottschall, S.J.
Francis T. Hannafey, S.J.
Simon G. M. Koo
with
Gianni Criveller

The Beijing Center Publication Series

[2019–04–GHKC]

ISBN: 978-1-7337899-0-5

PUBLISHED BY THE BEIJING CENTER PRESS, CHICAGO, ILLINOIS, USA

The Beijing Center
北 京 中 国 学 中 心

WWW.THEBEIJINGCENTER.ORG

First printing, April 2019

Front Cover Photo Credit:
Ignoto, Ritratto di Padre Matteo Ricci, sec. XVII – Olio Su Tela, 110 x 90 cm.
Photographic Archive of Macerata Musei Civici di Palazzo Buonaccorsi.
Book cover photo image used with permission.

Contents

6

Dedicated to the late Dr. Stephen Freedman

(1950–2018), global education innovator

and a good friend of TBC.

Foreword

Late in his life Matteo Ricci wrote a journal based on his memories. But his letters are more direct, more intimate. The few letters reproduced in this volume — to superiors, class mates and family — open a window into his mind and heart. They reveal his dreams, joys and disappointments during his long journey in China. Along with pride in his achievements, satisfaction at his mastery of the Chinese language and joy in his growing bonds with important Chinese scholars, Matteo Ricci's letters reveal his vulnerability, loneliness, melancholy and sheer physical fatigue.

More than 400 years since the death of Matteo Ricci, we are still gaining insights into his personality, his friendships, and the fascinating world in which he lived. This book of selected translated letters of Matteo Ricci and comments on them, prepared with care by scholars associated with The Beijing Center, will help us gain a deeper appreciation of the person Matteo Ricci, and of the human context of his intercultural encounters.

The famous Jesuit pioneer arrived in China in the late Ming dynasty. Others from the West had failed to meet or understand Chinese people or culture. Ricci was instructed to know well the Chinese language before entering into his mission. This was but the first step. With enormous intelligence, flexibility, cultural sensitivity and sheer humanity, he earned the respect and friendship of members of the Confucian literati.

In his letters he appears not so much sent, but drawn in faith deeper into his mission. Nor is this simply his own path. His constant flow of letters, only a small number of which have yet been recovered, reveal that he was intent on building a corporate mission. For this he charted a strategy for cultural accommodation that was long term, wise and open minded.

From any perspective, Matteo Ricci's achievements were prodigious. Ricci's life work was to build a bridge between Chinese and European cultures, and between Confucianism and Christianity. To gain the respect of the Chinese literati he realized that he could introduce astronomy and mathematics, gaining respect, for example, through reform of the Chinese calendar. Indeed those who followed him could fulfil this dream.

Matteo Ricci sought first to understand and to befriend others. A towering figure, yet somehow vulnerable, his persistent, humble example may guide and encourage us today when intercultural accommodation remains a challenge to many.

Mark Raper, S.J.
Chair of the Board of Trustees
The Beijing Center

Preface

The letters of Matteo Ricci (1552-1610) provide insight into the thinking and experience of this highly regarded Jesuit scholar and missionary. From the time of his first arrival to Macao in Southern China in 1582 to his death in Beijing in 1610, Ricci composed many letters that offer an important a personal and intimate look into his activities and his gradually developing understanding of China and the Chinese people. Fifty-four of the letters written by Ricci have survived to the present day; six from India, two from Macao, and the rest from China. While Ricci's well known work in cultural and intellectual engagement with China is often described as successful he also encountered many personal difficulties, setbacks, and challenges. The letters provide us with rich insight into Ricci's life, his work in China, and show much wisdom based on real experience of both success and at times failure in an effort to achieve positive cultural engagement and understanding.

There has been extensive study of Ricci's life and his work in China. Scholars have also carefully studied Ricci's original writings in Chinese and in other languages. While in recent years translations of Ricci's letters have appeared, there is less scholarship in the English language on the letters to date. This publication is an small step toward the larger project of publishing a scholarly edition of all of Ricci's extant letters translated into English with commentary.

In 2011, The Beijing Center for Chinese Studies and The Beijing International Society published *Matteo Ricci: Five Letters from China* edited by Gianni Criveller. This publication translated into English for the first time five of Ricci's letters and provided critical analysis and commentary. This earlier project was part of an effort to celebrate the 400th anniversary of the death of Matteo Ricci in 1610. The 2011 publication is included in full here. This present revised edition also includes four new translated excerpts of letters by Ricci written from China during significant periods of his life, along with six articles contributed by Ricci scholars and others with direct experience of China. In addition to new scholarship in the contributed articles and English translations this book presents extensive commentary, information about background and context, and biographical notes on some of the persons mentioned in the letters. This edition also provides a useful chart with basic information on all of Ricci's 54 extant letters.

The essays in this collection consider Ricci's letters and their significance from multiple perspectives. In "The Return of Ricci's Letters to China" (pp. 25–30 in this volume) Thierry Meynard explores the fascinating translation and publication history of the letters and astutely observes that the letters have now returned to China with the appearance of a complete translation into the Chinese language. Meynard notes well that the letters "today bring with them all the subsequent history of a mutual encounter" and suggests that Ricci himself would be surprised that his letters are now translated into the Chinese language. Meynard notes further that Chinese readers as well as readers in the West would benefit from Ricci's approach to cross-cultural engagement and mutual understanding.

Michela Fontana in "The Role of Ricci's Letters for my Work as Biographer" (pp. 31–34) offers reflections on the ways the letters helped her prepare a major biography on Matteo Ricci. Fontana points out that letters can assist a biographer to better grasp the "personality... emotions, and small facts of everyday life" of a protagonist. Fontana observes that Ricci's letters helped her learn more about his emotions, his cultural development, and scholarly and missionary work. From another angle, Fontana suggests that the letters "allow the reader to 'discover' China with Ricci."

Those who have had extensive time living and working in China will most surely identify with Eugene Geinzer's inspiring

"A Chinese Correspondence that Ricci Began" (pp. 35–40) written in the form of a letter. Geinzer lived and worked in Beijing for more than 12 years and he finds inspiration and parallel with Ricci's experience and his own. For Geinzer, the study of the Chinese language, his own professional engagement with Chinese architecture, and the gift of human friendship helped him understand Ricci's experience, 400 years later. Geinzer's letter will surely enlighten present day travelers to China.

Amy Yu Fu in her timely "An Odyssey of Interreligious Dialogue: Rethinking Matteo Ricci's Mission to China" (pp. 41–50) considers the necessary conditions for effective dialogue and engagement with religious others which she finds present in Ricci's China enterprise. Fu identifies transformation by learning, commitment to friendship, and pursuit of interconnectedness as essential for genuine interreligious dialogue. Fu's thoughtful study explores these subjects in light of Ricci's work and observes that Ricci's "admiration for Chinese culture is sincere" while at the same time is grounded in his fundamental missionary enterprise. Fu proposes that Ricci's openness to learning, friendship based on respect and trust, and the pursuit of interconnectedness are necessary elements in genuine inter-religious dialogue.

Antonio De Caro in "Matteo Ricci and his Personal Letters: A Breach in Ricci's Existential Journey" (pp. 51–60) looks at Ricci's personal life and the particular human challenges he faced during his years of work in China. De Caro's creative study explores the existential and oneiric (pertaining to dreams) dimensions of Ricci's life while also drawing on Ricci's journals. De Caro's essay examines Ricci's own human path by exploring his ideas, hopes, dreams, and struggles, which help us better understand the author and his context.

Jean-Paul Wiest's comprehensive essay "Matteo Ricci: Pioneer of Chinese-Western Dialogue and Cultural Exchange" (pp. 61–71, written in 2010) provides biographical information on Ricci and considers his pioneering work in dialogue and cultural exchange. Wiest's essay first appeared in the predecessor to this volume and it presents the background necessary to understand Ricci's significance for today.

This project initially emerged from the conviction that Ricci's letters have value for readers today. In his correspondence with Jesuit superiors, family members, friends, and associates, Ricci's personality and determination shine through clearly. In fact, many of Ricci's letters sound surprisingly contemporary and are rich in wisdom and grounded in real experience. They are helpful examples considering the deep challenges of cross-cultural understanding and engagement today. Ricci wanted to understand and grow in his own enduring engagement with China. He knew that he needed to learn the Chinese language, intellectually engage the literati, scholars, and others of the Ming period, and by so doing he entered into deep friendship with many Chinese people. Many of the things that Ricci loved (e.g. learning, science, friendship) were also loved by the Chinese people. These and other values in ancient Chinese culture perdure to this day. This book explores Ricci's thought as revealed in his letters and demonstrates that, even in the face of today's complex and unique challenges, he can continue to guide and inspire us.

Introduction from the 2011 Edition

Gianni Criveller

Matteo Ricci's letters are exceptionally important for understanding Ricci's personality, his own perception of peoples and events, the progress of his missionary enterprise and the rationale of his strategic decisions. But only few scholars and readers have been able to access this informative mine.

Fifty-four letters by Matteo Ricci have survived to the present day. Six of them were written from India, two from Macao, and the rest from China. Forty-eight of his letters are written in (sixteenth century) Italian and six in Portuguese.

Ricci's letters are presently available in two Italian publications. The first one was edited by the early twentieth century Jesuit historian Pietro Tacchi Venturi[1], and the second publication is by Francesco D'Arelli[2].

A significant number of Ricci's letters have been lost. While only two letters I to Valignano have survived, their content clearly indicates that the correspondence between the two missionaries was frequent. It is fair to assume that Ricci might have written a letter every month to Valignano for a period of about 20 years. And the same can be said about letters he sent to his family and friends, such as Martino de Fornari, Nicolo Bencivegni, Fabio de Fabii and others.

Even more regrettable, Ricci's entire Chinese correspondence has been lost. In (D'Elia, 1942, p. 1608), Ricci wrote to Superior General Claudio Acquaviva as follows:

One of the major occupations of mine in this land is to answer, in Chinese, the letters I continuously receive from various places and from

[1] Venturi, P. T. (Ed.) (1913). *Opere storiche del Padre Matteo Ricci, S.I.*, Macerata. Giorgetti

[2] D'Arelli, F. (Ed.) (2001). *Ricci: Lettere (1580-1609)*, Macerata. Quodlibet

important people. People I have met long ago or even people I have never met, who nevertheless write to us because of our good reputation[3].

[3] Ricci to Acquaviva, Beijing, March 8, 1608.

Unfortunately not even one of these letters (there must have been a few hundred) have surfaced so far.

The bibliography on Matteo Ricci is quite extensive. Some of Ricci's letters, or their passages and sections, have been translated into other languages, such as English, French and Chinese. However, to the best of our knowledge, the five letters that we present here were never translated into English or other languages before.

Five Letters

The five letters we present here are specifically selected for the following reasons. We start with the first letter Ricci wrote from Chinese soil, *i.e.*, Macao, dated February 13, 1583. It is followed by the first letter Ricci wrote to his superior general, Claudio Acquaviva, dated November 30, 1584. Even though it was written in Guangzhou, the letter is a review and a commentary of his first year in Mainland China, spent, as is known, in the city of Zhaoqing. These two letters represent Ricci's opinion and impressions at the beginning of his Chinese enterprise. They are important and insightful to know how he perceived himself at the beginning of his mission, and how he perceived Chinese people and culture, things and events around him. We notice that Ricci's initial approach was, after all, somewhat traditional, and he expressly states the religious intention of his presence in China. He holds an opinion on the supposed easiness of converting the Chinese that will change with the passing of the years. He describes Chinese language and things, peoples and events in a way somewhat confused and imprecise, often making comparisons with his native culture. It is a typical outlook of those who enter into a different culture. In an important sense, in these two letters we see Ricci going through what sociologists refer to as "culture shock."

The subsequent letters written after many years in China, and his account, written in the last two years of his life, entitled *On the Entry of the Society of Jesus and Christianity in China*, reveal how Ricci progressed in his understanding of Chinese things; his descriptions of language, events, things and people will increase in accuracy and precision. But even in these two early letters we notice a self-evident fundamental intellectual honesty: Matteo writes only what he perceived and experienced personally. He realizes that his readers might have reservations and be incredulous about his narration, yet he is adamant in reporting things as they are. The third letter, to Girolamo Costa, dated August 14, 1599, was written from the city of Nanjing, the southern capital, and Ricci's fourth residence in the Mainland. The context is radically different from the two letters described above. Ricci has been in China for 17 years and founded four residences. He has even stayed in Beijing for two months (September 7 – November 5, 1598) and was a well-known figure in Chinese society. Yet, the true objective of his mission, to establish himself in Beijing to obtain permission from the Emperor for Christian preaching and security for missionaries and Christians, was not yet achieved.

Girolamo Costa was one of Matteo's closest friends. Their closeness was strengthened by two factors: they were both from the city of Macerata and both were Jesuits. We have six letters written to Costa, and here we translate the fourth one. The letters to Costa should be read with special attention because Matteo writes to him in an unconventional way, expressing things that he might withhold in official letters. For example, Ricci expressed his dismay at the inquisitional system: people who know nothing about China have the power to censor his Chinese books!

This letter is particularly remarkable as Ricci wrote with amazing clarity and openness about his missionary strategy. He rejected the criticism from those who pointed out that progress in China was much slower than in other missions. Ricci stated that influencing Chinese society as a whole was better than establishing small Christian 1 communities at its margins. Obtaining the trust and the approval of the central authorities was a prerequisite leading to mass conversions among the population at large. After securing the toleration of Christianity from the authorities, it would be safe to evangelize the population at large all over China.

The fourth translated letter is to Giovanni Battista Ricci, Matteo's father. Only five letters to family members are still extant, but the content of the existing letters indicates that Matteo wrote many more letters. Writing to his father from Beijing on May 12 1605, Matteo is not even sure whether he was still alive. In fact we also do not know that; we only know that Giovanni Battista was still alive in 1603. The literary genre of letters to his father is somewhat different from most other letters: here Matteo especially emphasizes the success of the evangelization and the good example of Chinese Christians. His father might have been less interested in social, ecclesiastical and political descriptions, but he would be able to relate to examples of Christian devotion. And Matteo anticipated his father's interest, offering some brief sketches of exemplary Beijing converts. Giovanni Battista, at the outset, opposed the vocation of his son, therefore narrating stories recounting the success of his preaching, Matteo might have wanted to reassure his father that his son's life was not wasted, but rather well spent for a great cause.

The fifth letter is the last of Ricci's extant epistolary. It is addressed to Portuguese Jesuit Joao Alvares and is dated February 17, 1909. This letter contains themes that are frequent in the letters Matteo wrote from Beijing. Ricci thanks João Álvares for the gifts he has received from Europe and asks for more. European scientific instruments, precious books, religious and artistic items were important tools, serving three purposes: tangibly impressing visitors by showcasing the quality of Christian and European civilization, practical instruments for transmitting European learning and strategic gifts for learned converts and high officials. Three objects deserve particular mention: the invaluable *Biblia Regia*, which survived a shipwreck; the Ortelius' *Theatrum Orbis* and the copperplate map of Ancient Rome.

Ricci mentions a very important letter he wrote to Fr. Francesco Pasio two days earlier. The letter to Pasio has survived, and might be considered as a testament of Ricci's mission method. Ricci mentions also two confreres working in China: Nicolò Longobardo, his successor, and Manuel Dias, responsible for the Nanjing residence. His last reference is to the heroic Jesuit brother Bento de Góes, who with this epic journey form India to

China confirmed Ricci's assessment that Cathy and China were one and the same land.

Finally, particularly important is the announcement that at the end of 1608 he had started "writing down the things of first event in the order that it occurred," and this, because "it came to mind that I am now the only one left of the first to enter this kingdom." And he was "especially dismayed at learning that the matters that I had to do with were described quite differently from how they really happened." Matteo refers to the composition of his very last writing: *Della entrata della Compagnia di Giesù e Christianità nella Cina* (On the Entry of the Society of Jesus and Christianity in China). Written from 1608 to 1610, the manuscript was brought to Europe by Nicolas Trigault. During his journey (1613–15), Trigault translated it into Latin and published it in Augsburg in 1615 under the title *De Christiana expeditione apud Sinas suscepta ab Societate Jesù* (*About the Christian Expeditions to China Undertaken by the Society of Jesus*).

Trigault occasionally changed the original (for example omitting the names of Chinese persons), and added substantial material from the 'Annual Letters' of 1610 and 1611 and information about Ricci's death and funeral, for a total of one fourth of the entire text. The Trigault/Ricci book was a great success. The second edition was published the following year (1616). We have a copy in the Rare Books Collection of the Ron Anton Library at The Beijing Center. The second edition was soon followed by various translations: French (1616, 1617, 1618, 1908), German (1617), Spanish (1621), Italian (1622), and English (1625).

Incredibly enough, Ricci's original manuscript was completely forgotten and was found only in 1909 in the Jesuit Roman Archives by Pietro Tacchi Venturi, and published by the same Jesuit historian in 1911. It was published again, with sumptuous commentary and annotations, by the Jesuit Sinologist Pasquale D'Elia from 1942–1949 under the title *Fonti Ricciane*[4], and it was a masterpiece of erudition.

Finally, in year 2000, Ricci's account was published again, this time in Macerata and with its original title[5].

Surprisingly, other recent editions in Italian (1983), French (1978), English (Gallagher; 1942, 1953, 1970), and Chinese (1983;

[4] D'Elia, P. M. (Ed.) (1942). *Fonti Ricciane*, Volume I, Roma. Libreria dello Stato; D'Elia, P. M. (Ed.) (1949a). *Fonti Ricciane*, Volume II, Roma. Libreria dello Stato; and D'Elia, P. M. (Ed.) (1949b). *Fonti Ricciane*, Volume III, Roma. Libreria dello Stato

[5] Corradini, P. (Ed.) (2000). *Della entrata della compagnia di Giesù e Christianità nella Cina*, Macerata. Quodlibet

a translation from Gallagher's English version) were based on Trigault's version, rather than on the original by Ricci. Even today, some writers quote from Trigault's version, seemingly ignorant of the existence of Ricci's original.

The five letters of Matteo Ricci presented here offer a good and comprehensive glimpse on how Ricci progressed in the perception and understanding of his mission to China, from the very beginning to the very end. I suspect that readers with the experience of a long sojourn in China will relate to his feelings and descriptions.

List of Ricci's Extant Letters

The following table lists the extant letters of Matteo Ricci, chronologically, according to the numbering system in the Quodlibet edition *Lettere*[6]. All references to letter numbers in this work refer to this numbering scheme.

[6] D'Arelli, F. (Ed.) (2001). *Ricci: Lettere (1580-1609)*, Macerata. Quodlibet

No.	Date	Written from	Addressee
1	18 January 1580	Cochin	E. de Goes
2	30 January 1580	Cochin	M. de Fornari
3	29 November 1580	Cochin	L. Maselli
4	30 November 1580	Cochin	G.P. Maffei
5	25 November 1581	Goa	C. Acquaviva
6	1 December 1581	Goa	G.P. Maffei
7	13 February 1583	Macao	M. de Fornari
8	13 February 1583	Macao	C. Acquaviva
9	13 September 1584	Zhaoqing	G. Román
10	30 November 1584	Canton	C. Acquaviva
11	20 October 1585	Zhaoqing	C. Acquaviva
12	10 November 1585	Zhaoqing	L. Maselli
13	24 November 1585	Zhaoqing	G. Fuligatti
14	30 September 1586	Zhaoqing	N.N.
15	29 October 1586	Zhaoqing	L. Maselli
16	9 September 1589	Shaozhou	A. Valignano
17	30 October 1589	Shaozhou	A. Valignano
18	12 November 1592	Shaozhou	F. de Fabii
19	12 November 1592	Shaozhou	G.B. Ricci
20	15 November 1592	Shaozhou	C. Acquaviva

(Continued on the next page.)

No.	Date	Written from	Addressee
21	10 December 1593	Shaozhou	G.B. Ricci
22	10 December 1593	Shaozhou	C. Acquaviva
23	12 October 1594	Shaozhou	G. Costa
24	15 November 1594	Shaozhou	F. de Fabii
25	29 August 1595	Nanchang	D. de Sande
26	7 October 1595	Nanchang	G. Benci
27	28 October 1595	Nanchang	N.N.
28	28 October 1595	Nanchang	G. Costa
29	4 November 1595	Nanchang	C. Acquaviva
30	12 October 1596	Nanchang	G. Fuligatti
31	13 October 1596	Nanchang	A.M. Ricci
32	13 October 1596	Nanchang	C. Acquaviva
33	15 October 1596	Nanchang	G. Costa
34	9 September 1597	Nanchang	L. Passionei
35	25 December 1597	Nanchang	C. Clavius
36	14 August 1599	Nanjing	G. Costa
37	2 September 1602	Beijing	N. Longobardo
38	? May 1605	Beijing	L. Maselli
39	9 May 1605	Beijing	F. de Fabii
40	10 May 1605	Beijing	G.B. Ricci
41	10 May 1605	Beijing	G. Costa
42	12 May 1605	Beijing	O. Ricci
43	12 May 1605	Beijing	J. Álvares
44	26 July 1605	Beijing	C. Acquaviva
45	26 July 1605	Beijing	G. & G. Alaleoni
46	15 August 1606	Beijing	C. Acquaviva
47	18 October 1607	Beijing	C. Acquaviva
48	6 March 1608	Beijing	G. Costa
49	8 March 1608	Beijing	C. Acquaviva
50	22 August 1608	Beijing	C. Acquaviva
51	23 August 1608	Beijing	F. de Fabii
52	24 August 1608	Beijing	A.M. Ricci
53	15 February 1609	Beijing	F. Pasio
54	17 February 1609	Beijing	J. Álvares

Acknowledgements

This volume is the fruit of much collaboration among many individuals and organizations. A particular thanks is owed to Gianni Criveller and those who helped to create the 2011 predecessor to this volume. Thanks also to the contributing authors who generously responded to our invitation. We are delighted to publish their new and original work hope that it will encourage future study of Ricci's letters.

Our heartfelt thanks to Thierry Meynard, S.J., who offered invaluable advice and encouragement especially at the early stages of this project. A word of thanks to Jean-Paul Wiest for his guidance and wisdom. Our thanks also to Ronnie Po-chia Hsia for his work and translation of Ricci's letters and also to the Hackett Publishing Company (Indianapolis/Cambridge) for granting permission to reprint the excerpts of Ricci's letters.

We would like to acknowledge Brian Mac Cuarta, S.J., and thank his team at the *Archivum Romanum Societatis Iesu* (ARSI) for research assistance and for granting permission to use photographic images of the original manuscript autographs of Ricci's letters held at ARSI. We also acknowledge the *Macerata Musei Civici di Palazzo Buonaccorsi* for granting permission to use the front cover image of the painting (held in their collection in Ricci's birthplace) *Ignoto, Ritratto di Padre Matteo Ricci*.

We also owe a debt of gratitude to Stephen Chow, S.J., for his ongoing generous support and encouragement of the work of The Beijing Center.

Finally, we are grateful to all of the faculty, staff, and students of The Beijing Center for Chinese Studies for their faithful companionship and encouragement.

The Return of Ricci's Letters to China

Thierry Meynard, S.J.

Ricci is famous today for his scholarly works, but only his letters give us a deeper sense of his rich personality. During his lifetime, some of Ricci's letters were already published in Europe, since the Jesuits in Europe systematically used letters from the missions to publicize their activities in foreign lands and to gain support. However, it was not until the early twentieth century that Ricci's letters began to receive serious scholarly attention. In 1909, the Jesuit historian Tacchi Venturi discovered in the Jesuit Roman Archives the Italian manuscript of Ricci's most famous work in the West, *Della entrata della Compagnia di Giesù e Christianità nella Cina*, previously known only through the Latin edition of Nicolas Trigault (1615). Venturi published the Italian original as the first volume of *Opere storiche del P. Matteo Ricci*[7]. Venturi understood well the close relationship between Ricci's work and the letters. He went on to collect the original letters and completed a scientific edition as *Le lettere dalla Cina* (published in 1913) which corresponds to the second volume of *Opere storiche*. This first edition includes 53 letters by Ricci. In this collection the first letter is written in Cochin, India (18 January 1580), and the last is written only a few months before his death (17 February 1609) in Beijing.

Venturi was a historian but was not a sinologist and he did not have extensive knowledge of the Chinese language. Upon returning from China, the Italian Jesuit Pasquale D'Elia went to Rome to teach missiology at the Gregorian University. D'Elia researched extensively and deeply the life and works of Ricci.

[7] Venturi, P. T. (Ed.) (1913). *Opere storiche del Padre Matteo Ricci, S.I.*, Macerata. Giorgetti

His *Fonti Ricciane* (1942-1949)[8] includes an annotated edition of Ricci's *Della entrata della Compagnia di Giesù e Christianità nella Cina* with many references to Ricci's letters, and until today, his scholarly work deserves to be consulted. Importantly, D'Elia identified many Chinese names which are mentioned only in a Romanized transliteration in Ricci's letters.

More recently, drawing on Venturi's edition Francesco d'Arelli edited Ricci's letters, adding an extra letter that was not included in Venturi's edition: this letter, number 15 in the Quodlibet edition, was written by Ricci to Ludovico Maselli on 29 October 1586 at Zhaoqing. This letter had been discovered and published in 1935 by D'Elia. Also, D'Arelli added to an appendix an extract from a letter of Ricci, written on 12 November 1607, which was quoted inside a Jesuit report for the years 1607-1608. To better appreciate the content of those letters, D'Arelli and other scholars added many notes, mostly drawn from those of Venturi and D'Elia, as well as a useful list of names with the Chinese characters. This second edition of the Ricci's letters was published in 2001 by Quodlibet at Macerata. Since the edition by Venturi is not easily found, the Quodlibet edition has today become the primary reference work for Ricci's letters, and can be considered the definitive work – notwithstanding a major new discovery of Ricci's in the future.

To commemorate the four-hundredth anniversary of the death of Ricci (1610-2010), some fifteen letters were translated from the Italian into French or English. The more substantial contribution was realized for the conference organized by the Ricci Institute of Paris in the headquarters of the UNESCO. For this occasion, eight letters of Ricci were translated into French by Jacques Gellard, S.J., based on the Venturi edition (corresponding in the Quodlibet edition to letters numbered 7, 19, 21, 31, 40, 42, 52 and 54). These translations were edited by Michel Masson, S.J. and appeared in *Matteo Ricci, un jésuite en Chine, Les savoirs en partage au XVIIe siècle* (Editions facultés jésuites de Paris, 2010). The notes by Venturi are also translated, and the editor also added other explanations and included original names in Chinese characters.

Also in 2010, The Beijing Center for Chinese Studies began

[8] D'Elia, P. M. (Ed.) (1942). *Fonti Ricciane*, Volume I, Roma. Libreria dello Stato; D'Elia, P. M. (Ed.) (1949a). *Fonti Ricciane*, Volume II, Roma. Libreria dello Stato; and D'Elia, P. M. (Ed.) (1949b). *Fonti Ricciane*, Volume III, Roma. Libreria dello Stato

work on translating and editing five letters (corresponding in the Quodlibet edition to letters numbered 7, 10, 36, 40, 54). The editor, Gianni Criveller, added many scholarly notes and also used Chinese characters for the names of persons and places. The work was published by The Beijing Center in 2011 with the title: *Matteo Ricci, Five Letters from China*[9].

Finally, at the occasion of the celebrations organized in 2010 by the Gregorian University in Rome, two letters were translated (corresponding in the Quodlibet edition to letters numbered 41 and 53) and are included in: *Matteo Ricci in China: Inculturation through friendship and faith*, edited by Christopher Shelke, SJ, and Mariella Demichele (Gregorian & Biblical Press, 2010).

Some forty years before 2010, celebrations were held in Taiwan the marking the four-hundredth anniversary of Ricci's entry into China (1584-1984). Following those celebrations, Kuangchi Cultural Group in Taipei published the Complete works of Ricci (*Li Madou quanji*, 1986) which includes the 53 letters of Ricci, translated into Chinese by Luo Yu. This publication did not include letter number 15 which is now available in the Quodlibet edition, but it did include letters by Michele Ruggieri and other Jesuits writing at the time of Ricci. The translation into Chinese of Ricci's letters by Luo Yu has been critically important for Chinese and Western researchers who cannot read the Italian, and also for those who did not have an easy access to the Italian original text before the 2001 Quodlibet edition.

The new Chinese translation of the 54 letters by Prof. Wen Zheng (Beijing Foreign Studies University) is an important milestone. Prof. Wen benefited from the help of Prof. Eugenio Menegon (Boston University) to revise his translation. Besides the 54 letters and one document in the appendix included in the Quodlibet edition, in this Chinese edition there are also two letters which have never been published before in any language. The first of these is addressed from Zhaoqing to Francesco Benci, and dated 20 November 1585; it describes the imperial examination system, and there is similar content in *Della entrata* (*De Christiana expeditione*, chapter 5 of Book 1). The second letter is addressed to Ricci's brother, Antonio-Maria Ricci, and is dated 12 December 1605. This letter is much more valuable in content

[9] The predecessor to the current volume.

since it describes Ricci's work in the capital. One point here deserves special attention. Ricci writes that in the past he did not consider it important to use Chinese rites, and therefore there was little result. But Ricci notes that he was now beginning to use Chinese rituals which are compatible with Christian doctrine and his identity as priest. Though Ricci did not mention what kinds of Chinese rites he was using, this letter shows that he was already using more indigenized expressions of the Christian faith. Those two additional letters were discovered by D'Elia and mentioned in his publication project. However, he was unable to complete the edition of Ricci's letters as planned. Menegon has retrieved these two letters and Wen Zheng translated them in Italian.

This second edition of the letters in Chinese was published in 2018 by Commercial Press (Shangwu yinshuguan) in Beijing. Now available with the same publisher are: *The True Meaning of the Lord of Heaven (Tianzhu shiyi)*, annotated by Mei Qianli, proofread by Tan Jie (2014, reprint 2015), and the Chinese translations by Wen Zheng of *Delle entrata* (2014), and Ricci's letters (2018).

I do not know Italian and therefore I am unable to judge the quality of Wen Zheng's translation compared to the one by Liu Yu. I only regret that there are very few notes which are too short, mostly drawing on the notes of Venturi, but without the context. With the development of Ricci studies, especially in Mainland China since the 1990s, there has been much progress in expanding and developing our understanding of Ricci and his interactions with the Chinese culture and society in his time. More than one hundred scholarly papers were produced investigating the Chinese interlocutors of Ricci: literati, court officials, Buddhist monks, etc. It is therefore quite regrettable that Prof. Wen did not make better use of the wealth of research accumulated in China in the last two decades. Prof. Wen had already translated Della entrata and he could have easily made cross-references with the letters, especially since Ricci drew much material from his letters to write *Della entrata*.

To illustrate this, I provide here only a few examples. When Ricci was still in Macao and had not yet arrived in Zhaoqing, he mentioned (letter 7) that Ruggieri was in contact with the

Tutano (dutang); but in the Chinese translation no note is given
to discuss the identity of the Tutano (Chen Rui). In the same
letter, Ricci mentions also a Spanish Jesuit coming with a group
of "capuccini" but no information is given on them, nor on the
Jesuit (Alonso Sanchez).

In another letter (21) written to his father from Shaozhou
(Shaoguan) on 10 December 1593, Ricci mentions that he is
expecting a companion. The Chinese translation fails to add
a note indicating that Ricci refers here to Lazzaro Cattaneo.
Also, in letter 52, Ricci mentions the coming of Bento de Goes to
Suzhou, but there is no footnote to give basic information about
this incredible travel of from India to Suzhou by land.

All the information otherwise given seems to me very sound.
I spotted only one obvious mistake. In the letter addressed to
Anonio-Maria Ricci on 12 December 1605, Ricci mentions that an
old man of more than sixty years old came to Beijing and was
baptized. In the note (p. 348), Wen Zheng indicates that this man
is Xu Guangqi. This is plainly wrong since Xu was baptized in
1603 (and not in 1604), in Nanjing (and not in Beijing), at the age
of 41 years old (and not over 60 years old), by the Portuguese
Jesuit João Da Rocha.

With this second Chinese edition, we can say that the letters
written by Ricci four hundred years ago are finally returning to
China. Return does not mean going back to an original position.
Indeed, both China and the West have changed significantly, and
I should say, have been greatly changed by each other. Ricci's
letters today bring with them all the subsequent history of a
mutual encounter that he pioneered, and with it also misunder-
standings and conflicts. Ricci probably never imagined that his
letters, which were after all addressed to family members and
fellow Jesuits, would one day be translated into the Chinese language. It seems to me that Ricci's letters are relevant for Chinese
readers in the present day because they invite readers to take a
necessary *détour* since truth is rarely accessed directly, but only
through the mediations of time, language and culture. Facing important and complex questions of the identity of Chinese culture
and of its relation to the West, readers can learn from Ricci's letters not only how he perceived China, but also what adjustments

he made to adapt to Chinese culture and society. In his letters, Ricci often wants to show how much progress he was making in his work of evangelization, how many people were baptized, how much respect and prestige was gained for the Catholic Church. In this missionary enterprise, it seems that Ricci is often driving his own path, but the letters also show Ricci being led by the Chinese: an official authorization to open a new residence in a particular place, invitations of the literati to interact with them, requests for sharing his knowledge in mathematics, etc. Ricci accepted these human mediations, quite remote from direct evangelization, because he believed that God was fully present in them. In this way, Ricci was gradually transformed by Chinese culture and by his Chinese friends, and understood that the value of his life was not based on how many Chinese he had baptized, or how many churches he had built. Ricci expresses clearly this spiritual awakening at the end of his life, when he writes on 22 August 1608 to Claudio Acquaviva, the Superior General of the Jesuits, that the success of the mission should not be evaluated from the number of Christians but from the foundation being established for something very big (letter 50). As Ricci was himself transformed by the encounter of another culture four hundred years ago, the letters he left us are an invitation for ourselves to also be transformed by a relationship which is beyond our own control.

The Role of Ricci's Letters for My Work as Biographer: Some Reflections

Michela Fontana

It is well known that one of the most valuable sources of information for a biographer are the letters written by the person whose life the biographer wants to depict in the most thorough and nuanced way possible. The biographer's work is devoted not only to providing an account in context of the protagonist's life, along with the meaning and significance of his work, but also to understanding and describing his personality, his emotions, and the small facts of everyday life. In this respect, dealing with a missionary living in China in the sixteenth century makes things especially difficult. First of all, Ricci's extant letters only total 54, a very limited number. And most of them are written as an essential part of his work, as part of his duty to inform his superiors (General Acquaviva, Visitor Valignano, Mission Superior De Sande, Vice Provincial Pasio) of the developments of the mission in China and to provide them with a description of a country mostly unknown in Europe. As a consequence the letters have a rather formal character. One letter written to Giambattista Roman from Zhaoqing (13 September 1584), is in the form of a short tractatus on China. The extant letters addressed to his brothers, former classmates from the Collegio Romano, and the five letters to his family (three to the father Giovanni Battista and one to each of the brothers Antonio Maria and Orazio) are where, moreso than in the other letters, Ricci expresses, albeit briefly, some of his emotions.

As far as the language is concerned, it should be noted that seven letters are in Portuguese and the others are written in a rather poor Italian, as is true for Ricci's journal (*Della entrata della Compagnia di Giesù e Christianità nella Cina*). Ricci is aware of this and he acknowledges to have lost the mastery of his own native language after many years of speaking Portuguese. This fact makes the reading not very fluent, rather laborious, and tones down the spontaneity of Ricci's writing. However, it also provides an additional indication of how difficult the work and life of an Italian missionary in China was in Ricci's day. All these relative limitations don't diminish the immense value of Ricci's letters. Ricci had such a charismatic and distinctive personality and this shows, even in the details and between the lines. The letters show his choices in coping with the difficulties he encounters, in directing with intelligence and flexibility his efforts to meet the goals of his mission, in dealing with his brothers, and with the members of the Chinese bureaucracy.

Even though Ricci's journal is still the basis for the mission's history, the letters have the specific value of being written while the experiences were actually unfolding and they give more directness, in comparison to Ricci's journal which was written during the last years of his life, based on his memories. The letters give more information and details on Ricci's experience and work. They help to follow the difficult progress in the building of the Chinese mission with its ups and downs. They also show Ricci's progress in the study of Chinese language, from difficulties to gratifications and help us to follow the slow change and improvement in his relations with Chinese people. We can perceive his growing familiarity with Chinese rituals, his incremental acquaintance with scholars and members of the imperial bureaucracy, his growing appreciation of their knowledge and wit ("The natural intellect of the Chinese is fine and acute" Quodlibet Letter 53). The letters allow the reader to "discover" China with Ricci, and to follow his growing awareness that China and Cathay were the same country, and how difficult it was for him to be believed in Europe.

The letters also show that his vision of the missionary work was advanced and open minded for his times. In a letter to

General Acquaviva from Goa (25 November 1581), he expressed his dissent when he learned that the Jesuit authorities had forbidden Indians, who were studying for the priesthood, from attending the course on philosophy and theology. In another letter from Beijing to General Acquaviva (15 August 1606) Ricci expressed his dissent to his companion Gaspar Ferreira, master of novices, who had not time to finish the course of theological studies, being barred by the regulations from taking the special Jesuit vow of obedience. Ricci often expresses his vision about how to put into practice Valignano's instructions to develop the Chinese mission and how cultural accommodation should evolve. Ricci often emphasizes that he cannot convert a higher number of Chinese as is expected in Rome. He outlines his strategy to proceed step by step, giving priority to conversions based on rational conviction. A recurrent topic in his letters is that he prefers to have "few but good" converts rather than "many and imperfect" (Quodlibet Letter 38).

Through the letters it is possible to understand more about the development of Ricci's cultural activities. The letters offer background on the preparation of his books in Chinese on ethical issues, the groundwork and writing of his Catechism (*The True Meaning of the Lord of Heaven*), and his comments on how these books were received by the literati and members of the imperial bureaucracy to whom Ricci was mainly addressing his work. Ricci aimed to build a bridge between Chinese and European culture, between Confucianism and Christianity, with the final goal being to bring his religious message.

The starting point of my interest in Ricci's life was his pioneering introduction of European science into China, an achievement that characterized the work of other Jesuits of the Chinese mission after his death. I found in the letters important details about how Ricci gradually realized that he could use European science and particularly mathematics and astronomy as means to gain the respect of the literati. Ricci, advised by the two prominent members of the imperial bureaucracy and converts Li Zhizao and Xu Guangqi, (two of the three "pillars" of Christianity in China, along with Yang Tingyun), decided to translate European books on mathematics and astronomy into Chinese. The most relevant achievement was the translation of the first six books of the *Elements* by Euclid with very close and invaluable collaboration of Xu Guangqi. In his letters, we see that Ricci was aware that if Jesuits with an expertise in astronomy were sent to China, they could help the Chinese to reform their calendar, thus gaining the respect of Chinese authorities. He repeatedly asked the authorities in Rome for this but his vision was to be fulfilled only after his death.

Concerning Ricci's emotions, the predominant attitude in his letters is optimism and the determination to achieve the goal of a successful mission. He expresses self-satisfaction for his achievements, for his mastering of the Chinese language, his growing familiarity and friendship with Chinese scholars, his rising reputation as a wise man, author of books and maps, well received by the scholars. But there are also moments of discouragement. In the first period of his life in China, Ricci expressed a deep nostalgia for the years he spent in Collegio Romano with his companions and teachers. In the following years – while he was getting acquainted with life in China – he expressed spells of sorrow, melancholy, feelings of loneliness and sometimes a sense of unfamiliarity towards China. As he grew older he often mentioned an increasing physical fatigue. The expression of melancholic emotions and fragility in the context of a general optimism and a consoling familiarity with his Chinese life is limited but meaningful. As a human being, Ricci is both proud and melancholic when he writes "Mi sono fatto Cina" ("I have become Chinese . . . ").

I close my remarks mentioning the letter written to his brother Orazio from Beijing (12 may 1605) where Ricci describes the life of a missionary in China in a very moving way:

> *"I remember writing in other (letters) to tell my brothers to think often of us priests living in these lands as in voluntary exile, far away not only from our loved ones, our parents, brothers, and sisters, and relatives, but also from Christian folk and our countrymen sometimes in places where not one European is to be seen for ten or twenty years... What then must be done by those who are at home with their families and friends in the midst of comfort and pleasure? ... I cannot in truth look forward to many years more and my hair is already all white..."*

A Chinese Correspondence that Ricci Began

Eugene Geinzer, S.J.

An Introduction to this Letter:

My trip to China in August 2006 was intended to be a six-month sabbatical. It lasted twelve years. From the outset I could not figure out what forces were holding me: the delight of oriental difference, or, the remarkable people I was meeting. I plunged into that conundrum trying to learn everything I could even while shaking off my Western biases. The resumption of teaching, after a six-year hiatus, could not have happened in a more ideal environment. The Beijing Center student is intensely curious, highly self-motivated and bright. What teacher could dislike that kind of student. I developed a new drawing course, "Seeing China Through Western Eyes," to teach standard drawing skills even while posing quintessentially China subject matter. I wrote a text book for that course. Then I tackled Ron Anton's choice topic, Chinese Handicrafts, drawing on the writings of John Dewey (who had taught the teachers of China) and Lin Yutang as philosophical and aesthetic substrates. All the while I accompanied our students on the big semester excursions and the Spring Break and Fall Break trips. Naturally fascinated by traditional Chinese architecture, I was shooting digital photos all the time. Eventually those photos and my research led to translating Liu Dunzhen's Zhong Guo Zhu Zhai Gai Shuo 中國 住宅概説 (An Overview of Chinese Domestic Architecture) from the French translation into English. When Dean Russell Moses asked me to consider teaching Chinese Architecture I jumped. I could have continued in China for another few years, but I knew it was better to get off the stage while they still liked me. Over the years the letters of Matteo Ricci have helped me reflect on my own experience of China. Following Ricci's lead I present here a letter which may offer guidance to other travelers to the Middle Kingdom.

Dear China Traveler,

   This first letter is more difficult to begin than I thought. Numerous spirits impede me, the most formidable is the Internet. Few of us sit down to compose reflective letters. Modern communication insists on immediacy, spontaneity and quick turnaround time. Another spirit that discourages my writing is the immensity of the transformative experience I had in China. A few paragraphs cannot contain what has happened. A comprehensive statement — the length of a book — would dissuade you from reading it. A third spirit frustrates me; it is the fact that I am a visual person who relies on first-hand drawings, photographs and measurements to record and report what I have seen.

   I begin where most travelers begin: with the Chinese language. Matteo Ricci puzzled over these obscure characters. Yet he mastered these "ideograms" in ten years such that he could read them upside down. Beginning at age 62 I knew I was "behind the eight ball," but I thought—given how visual Chinese is–my own pictorial mind would be of great advantage. Not so. I quickly became amused that one could take the character for "horse" 馬(ma3) to which one would add an Accent Aigu (') to form 烏(Wu1) "blackbird;" and then insert an inner eye in that blackbird to form 鳥(Niao4) "bird." What the image of a horse had in common with a blackbird, I had no visual clue. Yet I could imagine how a "blackbird" is related to the generic "bird." Still, phonetically, Ma, Wu and Niao perplexed me to the point of laughter and shame. Multiple analogs abound in the Chinese language. My visual gifts were hardly a help. What Ricci accomplished in ten years upside down, I could not get to the baby stage right-side-up in twelve years.

   My language teacher taught me an important lesson when I asked her, "How could it be visually possible, or, phonetically possible, or, anyway possible that there was a 'family resemblance' to these characters?" She responded, "There is no 爲甚麼 in Chinese." "There is no 'why' in Chinese." For us who are the progeny of Aristotle's "How, When, Where, Why, to What End, by What Means, etc." this was a sobering introduction to

Chinese culture.

Still the visual magic of Chinese culture snagged me. Trained as a ceramicist, wood sculptor, and architect, I spontaneously found my way to ceramic shops, carvers of tea scoops, and traditional architecture. On the fourth day of my "sabbatical", Father Ron Anton asked me to teach a course in Chinese handicrafts. Shortest sabbatical in years! I engaged my students to investigate parasols, musical instruments, basket weaving, peasants' shoulder yokes, village gates, hair combs, chopsticks. While they were on the lookout, I photographed every "unique" thing I could not purchase. I hired masters to teach us kite-making and paper-cutting.

My greatest cultural breakthrough came when — realizing that I was not going to master Chinese characters at my age — I figured that I could elaborate a rich conversation with Chinese culture by studying Chinese architecture. While I knew nothing about "feng-shui," I quickly realized it is not nonsense to face a house south. It catches all the rays. But I was fooled — like most Westerners — by the imposing brick-red walls into surmising that they hold up these elaborate Chinese roofs; I was astounded to discover that these massive walls are not load-bearing, but merely screens to the elegantly efficient posts and beams which do all the work. Another surprise revealed itself. These tall columns and beams are intricately "mortised and tenoned" in such integral fashion that not a single nail or screw binds them. And that integrity holds yet another surprise: Chinese temples (and houses) are not "fastened" or embedded in the ground. In fact, because there is such seismic action in China, these robust columns and beams and rafters and purlins are so carefully interlocked that the whole structure literally dances like a spider atop the platform in the event of an earthquake. Those massive "screen walls" may crack and collapse, but the timber frame structure holds true. But what keeps this structure "grounded"? The weight of the roof. Yes, the weight.

There are even more surprises in the tiled gables and peaks that crown the temples with such color and fanciful verve. Of course they deflect wind, rain, and snow, but we typically don't think of solar power as a critical factor in roof design until the recent invention of solar panels. Well, in fact, Chinese roofs are about 2000 years ahead of the "green curve." Chinese peaked roofs are so arranged that the eaves that overhang the walls not only deflect rain water from striking the walls, but they also act like a sun-dial. To finesse the low thirty-degree winter sun they allow maximum sunlight to enter the elongated, shallow temple (or house) so that the winter's sun strikes and warms the rear-most wall. In the Spring and Fall these overhangs modulate just enough light of the forty-five-degree sun so as to slightly warm the cool rooms. But in the summer the overhang completely blocks the overhead sunlight from entering the house. Thus, the house remains cool in summer, warm in winter. One last detail I discovered that mesmerizes me: the upturned corners of roofs always seemed to me fanciful but functionless. Wrong! I detected their real function. The mid-morning or mid-afternoon winter sun rakes across the southern sky. At that point on the south façade where the overhanging corner of the roof would have diminished the sun's entrance, the Chinese builder ever so gently lifts up the corner so as to admit more light at that very corner.

You can imagine how I, a cabinet maker and architect, relished these discoveries. Not satisfied to photograph these architectural gems, I began to measure their dimensions with a laser measuring device, inspect the relationship of the screen walls to the vertical columns, and even inspect the eight coats of "horse hair-pig's blood-clay mastic" that protects these columns. I could not exhaust my thirst for new knowledge. Eventually I deployed my students to scout out and investigate traditional architecture.

Another aspect of my experience in China that fueled my love for the place was friendship. In his letters and journals Matteo Ricci writes beautifully about the centrality of human friendship during his experience in China. Friendship also became and remains an essential part of my own experience living and working in China. In time, a remarkable person entered my life. Not only was he astoundingly bright, but he was intensely invested in the subtleties of his culture. Being a "foodie", he helped me taste-test Tibetan, Uyghur, Shandong, Yunnanese, Sichuanese cuisine and that of his mother's own kitchen. Knowing my love for music he took me to Chinese

Opera and searched out hidden indigenous music bars to expose me to new sounds. Since he knew my low tolerance for Karaoke; once he chided me, "You stayed the whole three hours!"

Justin Zhao became my alter ego, a kindred spirit, my "vade mecum." In most typically and abruptly honest Chinese fashion, he would correct me were I to make some wrong assumption or utter some naïve opinion. He was so eager for me to know the real China. As I departed to Hong Kong for heart surgery in October 2006 Justin presented me Lin Yutang's "My Country and My People" with these words, "Though written in 1935 this is the most accurate portrait of Chinese Culture." I could trust his opinion because Justin had read everything . . . I mean, "everything" about his culture. Even as I was taken aback by his directness, I was overwhelmingly charmed that he was determined to be fiercely honest. If he knew something, he knew it. If he didn't he was just as honest, "I don't know that."

One summer, knowing how much I loved Chinese architecture, he played my "Cicerone," escorting me to Datong, Pingyao, Taiyuan then down to Anhui Province to see the "Salt Box" houses. Justin concluded the tour by asking me, "Which would you prefer to live in?" On another adventure he introduced me to the glorious "donut-shaped" houses of the Hakka. Still another trip exposed me to the fantastical Feng Yu Qiao "wind and rain bridges" of the Dong people.

During the arduous but thrilling adventures of the two-week-long Silk Road Excursion, the Fall Break trip to Guilin, the Spring Saga of the Yunnan Excursion and the Spring Break trip to Sichuan or Fujien, Justin would nudge me along in my "espionage," (as he would call my minute measurements of Confucian temples and Tibetan houses.) He would deflect the guard's attention and give me camouflage to do my work. At one point the guard spied my red laser beam. Fearing I was caught out, Justin approached me to try out the device himself, giving me some cover. We measured a remote ceiling of the Beijing Confucian Temple.

While his mother is a great cook, his step-father is the painter of fabulously large "portraits of Chinese villages." When he could discern my whole-hearted resonance with his father's art,

Justin asked me to write an appraisal. I did it gladly. When his exhibition moved to the The National Gallery of Art in Beijing the curator translated my words into Chinese—and then excised my name. That was a lovely compliment; I would rather be recognized for the acuity of my understanding of another's art than for my name.

Eventually I had accumulated so many plans and documents and photographs of traditional Chinese architecture I could teach a course. How implausible that I, a foreigner, could begin to comprehend this great architecture that only in 1894 was surpassed by the fire-proof structural integrity of the Reliance Building in Chicago.

China has transformed me in unobservable ways. Now I know what Both/And really means. One can be as direct as Justin's correction and as indirect as Justin's self-effacement. I understand that you can hold opposite opinions without feeling contorted. Sweet and Sour is not so strange. Now I know that you do not have to speak; that silence is often a full statement. Yin and Yang are complete opposites that hold their own opposite within. Intense sadness and deprivation can be very funny. Chinese movies such as "King of Masks" prove this. I try to resist asking, "Why?"

When you visit any part of China you can use your own tools to penetrate this ancient, rich, and complex culture. Your capitalistic opportunism will mesh with the clever food wagon merchants who pop up at meal times and flee when the police prowl. Your chromatic scales learned in choir or through iTunes will detect a soul-mate in a jazz club who can teach you how to hear one-quarter and three-quarter intervals on his guzheng. Scout out some 'hutong' that intrigues you, follow its sinuous path, and discover a Chinese village that will captivate you for many years.

Eugene Geinzer
24 February 2019

An Odyssey of Interreligious Dialogue – Rethinking Matteo Ricci's Mission to China

Amy Yu Fu

Introduction

A brief glance at the biography of Matteo Ricci (1552-1610) highlights the uniqueness of his position in Sino-Western history. Never before has any Westerner left such a profound and lasting impact on Chinese culture. As one of the earliest and foremost members of the Jesuit China Mission, he introduced Western science and technology, composed a catechism in Chinese, compiled literary treatises on topics ranging from friendship to morality in Chinese, and most importantly, befriended a large number of brilliant Confucian literati of the late Ming society. He had, in the words of Pope John Paul II, "opened the path between East and West, between Christianity and Chinese culture."

Ricci's life and work have been narrated over and again in numerous historical writings. For some, he embodies the generation of giants who are endowed with "monumental patience and exquisite tact" in hagiographical writing[10]. Others deem Ricci and his confreres opportunistic and expedient at best, imbibed the naïve belief in the compatibility between ancient Chinese ideas and those of the Bible[11]. Still others assert that the Jesuits play the role of exotic purveyors of curiosities, intended only as a means to an end — the conversion of Chinese[12].

[10] Dunne, G. (1962). *Generation of Giants: The Story of the Jesuits in China in the last Decades of the Ming Dynasty*. Notre Dame, Indiana: University of Notre Dame Press

[11] Gernet, J. (1982). *China and the Christian Impact: A Conflict of Cultures*. Cambridge, U.K: Cambridge University Press

[12] Xia, G. (Ed.) (1996). *Sheng Chao Po Xie Ji*, Hong Kong. Alliance Bible Seminary

Multiple layers of interpretations of Ricci's role during the late Ming have been added for centuries, to the extent that the original picture of the man tends to be fragmented and faded. Was Matteo Ricci a sincere admirer of Chinese culture or merely "cloaking himself in the trappings of Confucian tradition?[13]" What did he attempt to achieve in his engagement with Chinese? How did he come to be a cultural broker between East and West? Was his evangelization a "marvelous failure" in terms of the number of converts? One might even wonder, in modern parlance, how Ricci could maintain the delicate balance between creative openness to religious others and commitment to his home tradition in his interreligious encounter?

[13] Levenson, J. R. (1964). *Confucian China and its Modern Fate*, Volume 3. Oakland, California: University of California Press

These questions are, needless to say, relevant in today's religiously pluralistic world. On the one hand, reflecting on Matteo Ricci's experience helps us identify who he and his contemporaries were, Chinese or Europeans in a collective sense, and to a lesser extent, who we are, through this shared historical and cultural heritage. On the other hand, as a crucial figure in the early phase of Chinese-Western relations, Ricci's dialogical Odyssey strongly suggests how genuine dialogues between people of different faiths and values may be facilitated and fostered.

I argue that there are three demanding conditions for an effective dialogue and engagement with religious others that is persistent throughout Matteo Ricci's missionary enterprise: the transformation by learning, the commitment to friendship, and the pursuit of interconnectedness. Below I shall discuss these conditions, focused primarily on Ricci's letters and other works.

The Transformation by Learning

The rule of the sixteenth century was Euro-centrism where a sense of superiority was deeply ingrained in the European mind. Most, if not all, missionaries then held no interest in the religion, philosophy and language of other cultures. It was the rare genius and insight of the Jesuit Visitor-General Alessandro Valignano that figured prominently in developing the unique adaptive approach to proselytizing in China (Dunne, 1962, p. 17).

When Matteo Ricci arrived in Macau to join Michelle Ruggieri, learning Chinese and preparing for the entry to Guangdong, he observed that there were few learned priests in Macau. In a letter to Superior General Claudio Acquaviva in 1583, Ricci reported that the Portuguese Jesuits not only had no interest in converting the Chinese, but that they also despised Ruggieri for his three years of almost exclusive study of Chinese, which almost "turned him into a martyr." It seems that the Portuguese thought language study unnecessary and irrelevant to priestly duties. Ricci commented specifically that only those who were directly involved knew what it meant to be a missionary (Luo, 1986, p. 41).

Ricci began his language study upon landing in Macau in August (1582). Six months later writing from Zhaoqing, Guangdong, he reported on some progress but described the language as complicated, lacking the use of article, gender, and case, etc. (Luo, 1986, p. 32) Three years later (1585), Ricci claimed that he could converse without interpreters and write and read simple Chinese[14]. In another letter to Ludovico Maselli the same year, he mentioned that he was able to preach fluently. However, Ricci preferred writing to preaching as "in China one can achieve more with books than words" because the Chinese held high esteem for printing books. Second, the written system in Chinese works more effective than that of the phonetics, which is more confusing in tonal variety. He was, therefore, more competent in conveying religious messages through writing.

Because dialects varied from province to province, while written language is the same nationwide and applicable in the Sinitic world, the early Jesuit language program adopted spoken mandarin and highlights reading and writing[15]. Liam Brockey's study expounds that the Jesuits "did more than seek a passing fluency in Mandarin... the years spent... imbued them with... admiration for... Chinese thought (Brockey, 2009, p. 255)." A letter by Joao Monterio claimed that the study of Chinese books helps "to find pearls of wisdom so full of honey and so covered with the sugar of divine consolation... that the priest derived more pleasure than Poets in the lessons of their Homer or Virgil, the Rhetoricians in their Cicero and Lucian... (Brockey, 2009, p. 255)"

[14] Ricci should have learned mandarin, which is used among scholars and officials during his time, and this spoken language was accessible to the majority of Chinese.

[15] In contrast with the Jesuit strategy, the Dominicans seemed to lay less emphasis on language learning. During the Chinese Rites Controversy in late seventeenth century, the then Vicar Apostolic of Fujian Charles Maigrot was rebuked by Emperor Kangxi as an outsider who dared to talk about insider issues since he was unable to speak and barely read any mandarin, though he has been in China for a few years. Maigrot was, in fact, able to speak the Fujian dialect.

Ten years passed before Ricci declared to Acquaviva that he
had found a learned Chinese teacher finally, mocking himself
a young pupil in this "old" age again. He was then translating
three of the Confucian Four Books into Latin and continued
revising the new catechism *The True Meaning of the Lord of Heaven*
(*Tian Zhu Shi Yi*, TZSY). Except for the charting of his popular
world map, Ricci published most of his works after 1595, such as
On Friendship (*Jiao You Lun*, 1595), *Tian Zhu Shi Yi* (1603), *Twenty-
Five Sayings* (*Er Shi Wu Yan*, 1604), *Ten Essays on Extraordinary
Men* (*Ji Ren Shi Pian*, 1608). During the last nine years of his life
in Beijing, he had once asked to be removed of his administrative burden to devote more time to writing but failed. In those
productive years, Ricci was increasingly proficient in integrating
Confucian ideas with Christian doctrines in his Chinese work.
Inarguably the preliminary and advanced study of Chinese
language and classics is critical to the formation of Ricci as a
competent cultural mediator. A Chinese friend portrayed him
thus: "when at his residence, Ricci always holds a book in hand,
and his memorization is fascinating (Zheng, 2003, p. 190)." Not
only did the lifelong-learning attribute to Ricci's growing appreciation of the Chinese culture but also changed his perspective of
the direction of the mission[16].

Writing to Acquaviva in 1584, Ricci concluded his letter by
referring to the danger of his work (those "discourtesies, insults,
and attacks by the local residents in Zhaoqing") and the diffi-
culty of conversion. He offered, however, to stay in China out
of obedience, alluding to his discouragement and frustration
at the time. Almost eleven months later, writing to Acquaviva
again, he stated his progress in language study, and the charting
of the world map that was going to win him immediate acclaim.
This time he expressed his willingness to stay for long. When the
Jesuits were almost driven out of Zhaoqin to Macau in 1589[17],
Ricci described the blow as if the rock of Sisyphus rolling down.
Nonetheless, he promised to work "another seven years for
Rachel" when they managed to stay in Shaozhou three months
later.

Upon entering Zhaoqing in 1583, Ricci was optimistic about
conversion, he anticipated large number of converts soon be-

[16] Modern scholars are
aware of the appreciation
that Matteo Ricci had for
Confucian philosophy
which is not shared by his
successors who spent less
time in language learning.
See (Brockey, 2009, pp. 253–
255).

[17] The new prefect sought to
confiscate the residence for
his personal use.

cause "the Chinese seemed not satisfied with their own religions at present (Luo, 1986, p. 83)." With time, particularly with the incremental growth of knowledge of the entire Chinese religious eco-system and social structure, Ricci recognized the immensity of the task. The Chinese would tolerate an enhancement to existing religious practices, but the Jesuits intended to dismantle the "idolatrous" traditions of their hosts. To reconcile the two conflicting religious views, Ricci had to fine-tune the Jesuits' missionary tactics to that of gradual permeation of Christian doctrines in the last twenty years of his life (Laven, 2011, pp. 66–67).

The Commitment to Friendship

The Jesuit position was not secure from the very beginning, for they had to rely on the protection of local authorities. This was further jeopardized by the three-year rotation of officials that characterized the Chinese administrative system. Earlier Michele Ruggieri was sent to Rome with a petition to have himself appointed papal ambassador to the Wanli emperor (1572-1620), but the arrangements never worked out. Unlike the Protestant missionaries that came to China in opium schooners and with gunboats in the nineteenth century, the Jesuits in the seventeenth century had nothing but themselves to rely on.

To dispel the suspicion of a people with deep-seated xenophobia, to thereby garner their respect and trust, and to save the soul of the Chinese eventually, Ricci needs to seek friendship from men of consequence. An early disciple of Ricci, Qu Rukui, a first level examiner from a distinguished family, turned up and later proved himself a loyal friend for life. For two years since 1589, Qu was an avid learner of Western mathematics, science and Christian doctrines. It was Qu Rukuai and the scholar official Shi Xing who recommended Nanchang, a center of learning, as a better residence than Shaozhou.

While in Nanchang in 1595, Ricci composed a short treatise on friendship (*Jiao You Lun, One Hundred Maxims for a Chinese Prince*) in the formal diction of classical Chinese. The 100 aphorisms were culled primarily from Greek and Roman authors, such as Plutarch, Aristotle, and Cicero. Ricci devoted much space in the essay to the ideal of friendship as exists only between virtuous men who love virtue for its own sake. *Jiao You Lun* was an immediate success upon publication, loved by Chinese intellectuals for centuries since it resonates, in many respects, with the Confucian views of friendship. Recent scholarship suggests that friendship was a popular topic among late Ming male-intellectual circles and Ricci benefited from participating in this discussion (Billings, 2009, p. 5). The essay seems to precipitate Ricci's successful networking with eminent literati ever since his days in Nanchang. For those who befriended Ricci, most admire his erudition in Confucian canons, European science and his virtuous lifestyle: celibate, pious, seeking not fortune nor fame but self-cultivation.

Before long, Ricci found himself among the learned scholars of the Nanchang elites, exchanging gifts and ideas of concern with each other: Western mathematics, astronomy, ethics and religion. In a letter to Duarte de Sande in 1595, Ricci wrote that it is preferable to preach among the intellectuals because he can teach self-cultivation and virtue. According to a survey by Lin Jinshui (Lin, 1987, p. 27), the number of Matteo Ricci's scholar friends whose name appeared in his letters amounted to 137. There are literati, military men, writers, historians, geographers, painters, and others on the list. Reading the name list looks like the Who's Who of the late Ming period. Interestingly, Ricci not only befriended Confucian scholars who promoted the "practical study" (Feng Yingjing) but also their opponents — followers of Wang Yangming (Zhang Huang) and Buddhist philosopher (Li Zhi).

While Ricci and Zhang Huang disagreed on ideas such as the origins of the universe, the existence of an omnipotent God, they did share a fundamental belief in the ethical ordering of society and the leading role of contemporary scholars' self-cultivation. As for Li Zhi, he had read *Jiao You Lun* before he first met Ricci in Nanjing. Clearly, he found in Ricci a kindred spirit as impressive and intelligent like no other. A certain poet named Li Rihua composed a poem for Ricci whereby we may see how the Chinese friend depicted him.

> *The rising sun dancing in the sea,*
> *The solitary waves travelling with rosy clouds,*

Riding sixty thousand li from the West,
A lonely raft floating to the East,
Life is but a brief sojourn,
Home is my abode of peace,
An unbearable dream of returning,
A sunny spring to the edge of the world.

Dialogues with scholars of various schools facilitated Ricci's entry into the literati circle, with it came respect and sincere admiration. Friendship, for Ricci, is never a one-way street where he gives all but receives nothing, for it must be reciprocal to be sustained. Nicolas Standaert described the relationship between the Jesuits and the literati thus: "the role of the [Chinese] Other in the formation of the identity of a group is... as important as the activity of the [Jesuit/European] Self itself (Standaert, 1999, p. 361)."

While many of the Chinese friends who quoted or printed Ricci's works revised them, the major Christian texts such as TZSL and TZSY were all refined and polished by men like Wang Pan and Feng Yingjing. Still others undertook to print Ricci's works or appended "flattering" prefaces to his works. Timothy Billings maintained that it is "helpful to bear in mind as a corrective to the familiar notion of the unique genius working in isolation... the very existence of the early Chinese translations of European scientific works to be a testimony of cross-cultural friendship itself (Billings, 2009, p. 13)."

The Pursuit of Interconnectedness

To gain a foothold in the Chinese religious world, the Jesuits, first of all, have to find their niche. To be sure, to be accepted as a religious newcomer, they would have to introduce some of the fundamental ideas of the Christian traditions to the Chinese in intelligible content, manner, and style.

The first catechism in Chinese — *True Record of the Lord of Heaven: A New Compilation from India* (TZSL), compiled mainly by Ruggieri, was published in 1584. In the book, the Jesuits referred to themselves as "bonzes from India" and made frequent use of Buddhist terminology, such as "jingshui (pure water), si (the

Buddhist temple), huayuan (alms begging). Further, they paid "scant attention to Confucian scholarship and totally ignores the existence of the religious aspects of Daoism (Lancashire and HU, 1985, p. 13)." Consequently the Jesuits were regarded by the local authority and residents as members of a Buddhist sect for a decade.

Although it is commonly asserted that Buddhism began to decline in importance from the mid-ninth century, Buddhism in late Ming continued to exert influence on various levels of the society. Nevertheless, Chinese Buddhism, as Erick Zürker asserted, "is not a philosophy but at heart a method, a system of well-defined spiritual practices considered ultimately to lead to liberation.[18]" In this system, the laity provide material support for monks while the latter provide ritual service for the former's accumulation of the merit in the karmic world.

Shortly afterwards, the Jesuits discovered that Buddhist monks were little respected in China and Confucian scholars looked on Buddhism as heterodox. Most monks, Ricci noticed, were illiterate and their lives akin to that of "social scum.[19]" A strong opposition to the superstitious Buddhist rites among the populace forged a bond between Ricci and some of his staunch supporters. In addition, in a letter Ricci mentioned that the emperor issued an edict to punish Buddhist priests for their public immorality, which severely threatened the existence of the Jesuit mission in Zhaoqing at one time.

Ricci abandoned the robe of bonze and dressed in the garb of scholars in 1595. He now identified himself with the literati, for he was indeed a scholar and priest from Europe. As such, the old catechism must be rewritten to remove its misleading Buddhist terminology. The first draft of TZSY, a treatise in the form of dialogue between a Chinese scholar and a Western scholar, was finished in 1596. Handwritten copies began to circulate among Ricci's friends to comment and preface. The book was officially published in Beijing in 1603.

Ricci's letter of 1595 to Acquaviva explained how he composed the new book. Studying the Confucian Four Books and Six Classics from learned teachers, he has found many ideas compatible with Christian doctrines: there is a Lord of Heaven, the

[18] Zürcher, E. (2013). Xu guangqi and his anti-buddhism. In J. A. Silk and E. Zürcher (Eds.), *Buddhism in China: Collected Papers of Erik Zürcher*, Leiden, Boston, pp. 567–583. Brill

[19] Yang Ching Kung has explicated the weakness of the structural position of Buddhist priesthood in Chinese society since the Song period of the eleventh century as follows: the absence of priests in most rural temples, the lack of centralized organization, inadequate financial position, and lack of organized laity. Further, the Buddhist monastic orders lack both participation in community charity and secular education. Buddhist monastic orders claimed a large number of converts from socially and economically helpless individuals, e.g. orphans and widowers, giving them in effect not so much spiritual as material salvation. Learned Buddhists are few in number and exceptions to the rule. In fact, a family would be despised by the community if Buddhist priest came to call frequently in addition to performing religious services. See (Yang, 1970)

unity of God, and the immortality of the soul (Luo, 1986, p. 209). The book was revised for a long time for Ricci was inspired by the many conversations and debates he had with scholars and Buddhist monks. While disseminating the Christian faith, Ricci was aware of the Confucian primary concern of moral self-improvement. Thus, as Lancashire has maintained, Ricci's purpose "from the beginning to the end, TZSY was to expound the nature of self-cultivation (Lancashire and HU, 1985, p. 22)." In the first part of TZSY, Ricci argued that the Chinese worshipped God in antiquity, but the learning and practice had been corrupted by later scholars with the introduction of Buddhism to China. Using natural reason and invoking Confucian classics, Ricci demonstrated the existence of an omnipotent God, Creator of heaven and earth, and the like. The second part attacked Buddhism, and the dialogues derived partly from his debates with Buddhist priests and laymen in Nanjing.

While the goodness of human nature, a favorite Confucian topic, was discussed, those doctrines such as incarnation and crucifixion, that which could not be illuminated by natural reason, was not. Likewise, he informed, in his early letter, that it is not necessary to send paintings depicting the Passion of Christ to China for no one could understand it then. Clearly, Ricci sought to accommodate his message to the Confucian literati, rendering TZSY a pre-evangelical work for catechumens or the curious one. Overall, the composition of the book, according to the Christian convert Xu Guangqi, is to "supplement Confucianism and remove Buddhism." In so doing, the Jesuits meet the so-called Chinese "cultural imperative" where a marginal foreign religion like Christianity must adapt to the orthodox Confucianism.

Despite the incommensurable difference between Confucianism and Christianity, Ricci took pains to build connections through the "common denominator" of ethics and moral cultivation. Although it took him a decade to forge the "right" link between Christian ideas and the Chinese recipients, the book and many other scientific works yielded fruitful results for the interreligious dialogue in the seventeenth century.

Conclusion

Reflecting on Matteo Ricci's Odyssey of interreligious dialogue, I have tried to expound that Matteo Ricci is, first and foremost, a Catholic priest of the seventeenth century, a product of his time. Through joy and sorrow and experiencing trial and tribulations, he sought to win the soul of China. There is no denying that Ricci was cloaking himself in the trappings of Confucian tradition. So too, his role of cultural broker was a magnificent "byproduct" of his missionary enterprise.

Nevertheless, to preach a new religion to another tradition, the language, culture, way of life and thinking of that tradition are but indispensable medium, without which genuine dialogue is beyond imagination. Religion simply cannot be transplanted entirely and directly into a new soil as if it could take root anywhere anytime for anyone. That said, Ricci's admiration for Chinese culture is sincere, though his was through lifelong learning, negotiating and interacting with the Other. Ricci's experience amply demonstrated that an openness to learning, the friendship built on respect and trust, and the pursuit of interconnection through common ground are critical to the peaceful coexistence of all.

Matteo Ricci and his Personal Letters – A Breach in Ricci's Existential Journey

Antonio De Caro

From the author: *Please note that the letters rendered here into English from Italian do not represent a final version of the translation. Moreover, I based my renderings on the Italian versions by (D'Arelli, 2001) and (Venturi, 1913) that I will mention afterwards in detail. Therefore, those renderings should be taken with a grain of salt and they are provided only to emphasize the relevance of the letters in order to unfold Ricci's personal ideas.*

Introduction

Fr. Matteo Ricci, S.J., (Li Madou, 利瑪竇 1552-1610) is probably one of the most famous Jesuit pioneers who arrived in China during late Ming dynasty. For this reason, scholars have been studying his writings and his efforts to establish a cross-cultural dialogue with Confucian literati. His zealous Christian life and his devoted study of the Chinese classics became an example for other missionaries. Yet, this image portrayed through the years lacks consideration of his deepest human sufferings that led him to embrace Chinese culture and Chinese philosophy. In Ricci's letters one can appreciate not only his exemplary character but also his human weakness, his daily suffering, and his concerns about the mission in China. Thus, his letters, that had been sent to several missionaries or relatives in Italy and elsewhere, narrate his periods of immense joy, his periods of profound suffering, and at the same time they elucidate several ideas that he developed during his journey. As a result, they are not solely relevant in order to study Ricci's personal thought but also, in a philosophical sense, they mirror his existential path that is the base of the ideas he developed during his stay in China.

There is another dimension expressed in his letters: Ricci's dreams. I attempt here to briefly describe not solely the existential portrait emerging from his writings but also the oneiric sphere, based on concrete dreams that he narrated to his fellow friends but also his hopes for the future. Therefore, I examine the philological problems that are part of the complex effort of rendering his letters into English and also the twofold dimension — the existential and the oneiric — emerging from his writings. I will explore only a limited part of the extended corpus of Ricci's letters and only few possible relevant topics. Yet, hopefully this would still be an example of their relevance in order to understand his personal adventure in China and his own creative mindset torn between a strong faith, a constant existential melancholy[20], and the fear of time running out, that is an invitation to reflect on the brevity of life.

[20] Criveller, G. (2014, May). The Dreams of the Melancholic Are True. Matteo Ricci's Ascent to Beijing. In *Beyond Thirty Nine. Hong Kong*. University of San Francisco

Rendering Ricci's Personal Letters into English: The Example of Gianni Criveller

A translation of several letters by Ricci into English has been completed by Gianni Criveller[21]. He rendered into English the following five letters: to Martino de Fornari (Macao, 1583), to Claudio Acquaviva (Guangzhou, 1584), to Girolamo Costa (Nanjing, 1599), to Giovanni Battista Ricci (Beijing, 1605), and to João Álvares (Beijing, 1609). For Criveller, the oneiric dimension of Ricci's life played a crucial role:

[21] Criveller, G. (Ed.) (2011). *Matteo Ricci: Five Letters from China*, Beijing. The Beijing Center for Chinese Studies (TBC)

> Ricci had a spiritual diary, yet it had been destroyed. However, the Chinese sources and the contemporary narrations on him show his heroic effort, that is spiritual, missionary and cultural, that led him to death due to his tiredness. In fact, Ricci had been a real 'martyr of friendship,' and he had been literally consumed for his friends. Furthermore, in the historical reconstruction he pointed out the central aspect of a dream he had on June 1595. In

that dream, Jesus, consoling him in a moment of deep personal crisis promised him that one day he would have arrived in Beijing. This dream is surely authentic (he narrated it six years before the actual realization of the prophecy) and it shows how Ricci lived his whole missionary experience under the guidance of Providence that guided and comforted him. Also, the category of the 'dream' as a divine indication is common not only to Ricci but also to other meaningful saints of the Church: St. Paul, St. Ignatius of Loyola and St. John Bosco.

The choice of the five letters had been addressed by Criveller as a description of Ricci's existential path, from the very beginning of his journey until his death. The first two letters according to Criveller "represent Ricci's opinion and impressions at the beginning of his Chinese enterprise." The subsequent letters express his late vision of China, his ideas, and his personal experience after his long journey on Chinese soil. Jean-Paul Wiest [in page 61–71 of this book] has pointed out that the one who had the initial idea to be fluent in the local language before any missionary activity was Fr. Alessandro Valignano SJ (Fan Li'an 范禮安, 1539–1606) whose method had been applied in China by Ricci. Therefore, the path of Ricci, also in the letters, represents not only his personal journey but also the work of the Society of Jesus on Chinese soil and the establishment of local Christian Chinese communities. Criveller provides a general picture of Ricci's personal change from his early attempts to his later judgments. In this regard, Criveller's work is an excellent example for any other possible rendering of the letters. At the same time, due to the difficulties of the enterprise it might be also seen as an initial work that can be critically discussed and further improved. Subsequently, I will point out the possible obstacles translating the letters into English.

The Linguistic and Cultural Challenges of Ricci's Letters

The distance between an educated reader and a text plays a major role in understanding the inner motivations of the author. In Ricci's letters this is evident. The 54 letters sent by Ricci in different languages, mainly in Italian, but also in Portuguese and Spanish, with quotations in Latin, portray a realm of words, sentences and cultural emphases that may not sound familiar to contemporary readers. One of the main challenges of translation is not solely to render the text literally but also to help the reader feel the same sensations and implied references emphasized by the author. Generally, several sentences or common sayings from the Latin tradition are present in the letters and they demonstrate the great erudition of Ricci in this regard[22]. Ricci adopted Italian terms in order to describe certain phenomena that he witnessed in China. For example, he refers to literati who had been successful in the imperial examinations as *dottori* as in the letter to Ludovico Maselli (Beijing, 1605). In another letter he explains all the terms in Chinese related to imperial examinations finding similarities in the Italian system as in the letter to Lelio Passionei (Nanchang, 1597). In places Ricci offers his own personal rendering of the places he had been as in the letter to Girolamo Costa (October 1595) where he explains the name of the court of Nanjing defined as the *corte di mezzo giorno* (the court of the South). The letters often clarify certain terms and adopt several quotations or references that are not necessarily familiar to the audience because of their personal content. In the Italian version especially well organized and curated by Francesco d'Arelli , these issues are widely discussed and this complete edition in Italian is a crucial and fundamental text for study of Ricci's letters[23]. This twofold dimension plays a crucial role in the relevance of this corpus.

Existence and Dreams in Ricci's Letters

Criveller has examined a particular prophecy that is crucial for Ricci's existence and a symbol of his genuine trust in the Lord's providence. This interpretation is pivotal in order to understand the unicity of Ricci's letters. They express his spiritual and existential journey in China with faith as the utmost shelter, helping him to survive and to continue his mission. Furthermore, in his letter to Girolamo Costa (Bejing 1605) he narrates another dream of Xu Guangqi 徐光啓 (1562-1633), a Confucian literato named Paul after his baptism:

He [*i.e.*, Xu Guangqi] told me, after our first meeting in Nanjing,

[22] For instance, in the letter to Girolamo Costa (Beijing, 1608), Ricci mentions a Latin sentence that would had been very familiar to the reader: *Omnia peccata sunt aequalia, Omnes sapientes et soli sunt liberi* (All the sins are equal and solely all the sages are free). This is actually a quote from Cicero even though in the original version is *sapientes omnes summe beatos; recte facta omnia aequalia, omnia peccata paria.* See (Reynolds, 1998, p. 158). Yet even an educated reader would feel unfamiliar with those sentences whether, for the addressee this sentence would have been of common knowledge. For this precise passage within Ricci's letters see (Bernard, 1937, p. 171)

[23] Sometimes, there might be discrepancies between the original manuscript and the Italian versions and this represents another obstacle for an accurate translation.

since he heard from me that we adored only one Lord, that in a dream he saw a temple with three chapels. In the middle one he saw an old man, and he heard that he was the Holy Father. In another [chapel] he saw another figure, and he heard that he was Holy Son and in the third one he did not see anything. For this reason, he started to adore the middle figure and the other one, in the other side; he did not adore the third because he could not see anything. Afterwards, when he had been catechized as a Christian he thought that the dream represented the Holy Trinity but he did not mention anything [about the dream] because they told him that Christians do not believe in them. Yet, during those days, when I told him that sometimes the Lord expresses his mysterious actions through dreams; then he told me what he saw and it seems that the Lord chose him as a firm column of the [Roman Catholic] Christian faith within those lands and he instructed him adopting a very special way[24].

[24] Translated from (D'Arelli, 2001, pp. 397–398) by the author

This episode is relevant for at least two reasons: first, here Xu Guangqi is depicted as the pillar of the Roman Catholic church in China and, second, it is through a dream that the literato imagined and saw the Holy Trinity and this is interpreted by Ricci as a dream given to him directly from the Lord. Yet, dreams in Ricci's personal letters are not only a positive sign for the believers but they are also seen as saving the Society of Jesus from enemies, as narrated in the letter to Giovanni Battista Ricci (Beijing, 1605):

Another Christian, falsely accused of theft and homicide, was imprisoned and he feared his cunning and powerful enemy. He had been aided with a great charity and support by Christians. However, because the judge was willing [to accuse him] providing an ambiguous sentence, during the night in front of him, in a dream, he saw Our [Lord] Jesus Christ. He saw His image in our residence, and He asked him the reason why he was not willing to help one person who was in trouble as a member of the church of the Lord. So, the day after, he absolved the Christian and he ordered to punish the accuser severely[25].

[25] Translated from (D'Arelli, 2001, pp. 390–391) by the author

At the same time, dreams in the letters have been related with the manifestation of evil, as in the case of the episode narrated by Ricci to To Fr. Claudio Acquaviva (1607):

The second [event] was that a woman, called Elena, saw in a dream a strange horrifying figure with a noose in his hand willing to stab her neck. She told him: "Go away because I am Christian and I follow the law of the Lord." The vision disappeared after those words. Afterwards, she had another dream: she saw the phantom two and three times, and she replied in the same way, and so at the end the monster said: "Because I cannot do anything with You, I will kill another person within the family on your behalf" and in the morning they found a gentile maidservant dead[26].

[26] Translated from (D'Arelli, 2001, p. 437) by the author

Dreams are widely present in Ricci's narration, both as a divine message or as a reference to the presence of evil in someone's life. They represent an important and very personal dimension of the letters, an intimate recall of the presence of the Lord especially when facing evil.

Furthermore, this is also a typical *topos* from the Latin tradition as well. For example, in the *Somnium Scipionis* (Scipio's dream), written by Cicero, a masterpiece well-known by Jesuits, Cicero wrote about a dream in which Scipio saw afterlife and talked about immortality of the soul. In this text Cicero writes: "[...] 'For the souls of those who have given themselves over to be the pleasures of the body, and have yielded themselves to be their servants, as it were, and the prompting of those lusts which wait upon pleasures, have broken the laws of God and man; when they have glided from their bodied, go groveling over the face of the earth; nor do they return to this place, except after many ages of wandering.' So he departed, and I woke from my dream![27]"

[27] Pearman, W. D. (Ed.) (1883). *The dream of Scipio Africanus minor*, Cambridge. Deighton

Ricci's dream, therefore, is also a metaphor of his existence as a dream, seeing in his path signs left by God and, following them, he had been assured that he would had been able to preach the Gospel. The dream is, in a nutshell, the symbol of the constant presence of the Lord in his life. So it is not merely a casual fact that another Jesuit missionary, Francesco Sambiasi (*Bi Fangji* 畢方濟, 1582–1649), as noted by Elisabetta Corsi, discussed dreams and images in his *Shuihua erda* «睡畫二答» (Two answers on sleep and images)[28]. This is part of a series of effort by the Jesuits to transmit in Chinese parts of the *De Anima* of Aristotle and other works on dreams and sensations[29].

[28] Corsi, E. (2012). Our little daily death Francesco Sambiasi's treatise on sleep and images in Chinese. In L. F. Barreto (Ed.), *Europe-China: Intercultural encounters (16th–18th centuries)*, Lisbon, pp. 79–96. Centro cientifico e cultural de Macao

[29] Meynard, T. (2015). The first treatise on the soul in china and its sources an examination of the Spanish edition of the lingyan lishao by Duceux. In *Revista FilosÃ§fica de Coimbra*, Volume 47, pp. 203–242

Another important element expressed in the letters is Ricci's

distress and personal suffering during his mission. One of the most evident examples is the letter to Orazio Ricci (Beijing, 1605):

> Truly I cannot think to live a long life, I'm completely hoary, and these Chinese persons are stupefied about my superficial old age [even if I am not so old], but they are not aware that they are the main cause of my white hairs[30].

[30] Translated from (D'Arelli, 2001, p. 401) by the author

In this passage, there is a confirmation of the theory supported by Criveller that Ricci had been a martyr of friendship. He was consumed by his devotion to his friends. In this passage we encounter the fragile soul of Ricci, his human suffering, and his personal distress that is part of his mission. His faith was based not only on a profound trust in the Lord's providence but it also emerged from his personal sorrow. This is clear in his letters as observed by Ronnie Po-chia Hsia:

> To convince his skeptical friend, Ricci turns to an extended metaphor: human life as a theater, full of sights and sounds, with all of us playing the roles of kings, ministers, officials, scholars, slaves, queens, concubines, and wives. But in the end, we, players one and all, will disrobe and leave the world the way we entered: naked and alone. Here, Ricci is adumbrating the great metaphor in European Baroque theater: the vanities of life, merely a stage of empty sights and sounds. The metaphor of theater also struck a deep chord in Chinese sensibilities, for the sixteenth century was the great age of Chinese drama and the development of the Kun opera: for there, in the realm of the Great Ming, the adopted home of the Jesuit missionary, the passions and sorrows of life were likewise played out on the dreamlike stage of human theater(Hsia, 2010, p. 234).

Here we encounter part of the Latin tradition that seems always present in Ricci's letters. There are at least two major Roman Latin philosophical topics in the letters and also in other works as noted by Hsia: the brevity of life and the necessary growth into old age. These two topics had been widely discussed in at least two great Roman Latin philosophical masterpieces; one by Seneca entitled *De brevitate vitae* (On the Shortness of Life) and another by Cicero, entitled *De Senectute* (On old age)[31].

In the former book, Seneca argued that "[...] many are kept busy either in the pursuit of other men's fortune or in complain-

[31] Hsia also argues that Ricci had been inspired by another the Sententiae et Exempla ex Probatissimis Quibusque Scriptoribus Collecta (Maxims and Exemplars Compiled from Writers Worthy of Approval) compiled by Andreas Eborensis, containing sentenes with classical Latin authors. See (Hsia, 2010, p. 155)

ing of their own; many, following no fixed aim, shifting and inconstant and dissatisfied, are plunged by their fickleness into plans that are ever new; some have no fixed principle by which to direct their course, but Fate takes them unawares while they loll and yawn—so surely does it happen that I cannot doubt the truth of that utterance which the greatest of poets delivered with all the seeming of an oracle: 'The part of life we really live is small.' For all the rest of existence is not life, but merely time.[32]" These classical ideas—life is short destiny and fate are stronger than life itself which will fade by the constant persistence of time—are discernible in Ricci's letters and is fundamental for both the authors. Furthermore, in the latter book, Cicero writes:

> [...] And, indeed, when I reflect on this subject, I find four reasons why old age appears to be unhappy: first, that it withdraws us from active pursuits; second, that it makes the body weaker; third, that it deprives us of almost all physical pleasures; and, fourth, that it is not far removed from death. Let us, if you please, examine each of these reasons separately and see how much truth they contain[33].

For Cicero, in a part of the dialogue *De Senectute*, old age is necessary and will always lead to unexpected and tragic events. For Ricci, much of his time had been devoted to serve the highest interests of the mission and he had spent his energies to establish a dialogue with his friends in China. François Xavier Dumortier has observed "being a friend of them, he could earn their friendship – not unlike the manner of Ignatius of Loyola and his companions who had become 'friends in the Lord'[34]."

Another frequent subject in Ricci's letters is the brevity of time. It resembles the ancient image of Cronos who is constantly eating his sons. For Ricci, time is constantly destroying his energies and he sometimes feels incapable of acting or continuing in his initial mission. As suggested by Hsia, Ricci had been continually addressing the vanities of life and he created a theater surrounding his audience. Yet, in his letters Ricci is the main character as he narrates his own adventure from a very different and unique perspective. The masquerade of existence comes to him as a mystery and only the light of faith is guiding him in his journey.

[32] Seneca (1932). *De brevitate vitae*. London: William Heinemann

[33] Cicero (1923). Cato maior. In G. P. Goold (Ed.), *De Senectute*, London. Loeb Classical Library

[34] Dumortier, F. X. (2010). Introduction. In C. Shelke, M. Demichele, J. Vila-Chǎč, and E. Ryden (Eds.), *Matteo Ricci in Cina. Amicizia e fede (Matteo Ricci in China. Friendship and Faith): Inculturation through friendship and faith*, Rome. Gregorian Biblical Press

As a result Ricci's letters are a complex and fascinating corpus of varied ideas and emotions that changed through his personal existence. They illustrate his strong faith and his personal sufferings, his tragic vision of the mission, and his trust in the Lord's providence.

Conclusion

"I confess to Thee, Lord, that to the best of my remembrance (and have often spoken of this), that Thy answer through my waking mother in that she was not perplexed by the plausibility of my false interpretation, and so quickly saw what was to be seen, and which certainly had not perceived before she spake even then moved me more than the dream itself, whereby the joy to that holy woman, to be fulfilled so long after, was foretold for the consolation of her present anguish."

– St. Augustine, Confessions, XI:20

Ricci's letters open the door to his personal ideas, hopes and dreams. In his own words there are present not simply events of his life but also his own existential path, suffering and joys, and a complete trust in the Lord's design. To adopt a metaphor, his letters are similar to a theatrical scene with several characters and Ricci plays different role but he is truly himself and therefore honest with his Jesuit brothers and his relatives. He is direct with his audience. Yet, in the end everything will be still be part of his mission and his personal journey because he is still full of hope and his personal sufferings are, for him, an evidence of his faith.

In this essay I attempt to show the relevance of Criveller's rendering into English of the five letters. Further, I consider the main philological and terminological problems present in Ricci's letters. At the same time I have focused on the twofold experience described by Ricci in the letters: a narration of his existence and of dreams. The former is related to his personal confession to his religious brothers and relatives of his weaknesses and his fear for the vacuity of life; the latter is related to his trust in the Lord's providence and his oneiric narration of the Jesuit mission in China. In the letters we find the most intimate portrait of a missionary who is guided by faith and by sorrow and, through his *via dolorosa*, his hard way, he has designed a new path for Jesuits to come after him. At the same time, the dreams he narrates in the letters are a sign of his personal and total faith in the messages given by the Lord. He felt closer to God in the dreams and this unique dimension is pivotal to reconstruct his own ideas and his biography.

Matteo Ricci: Pioneer of Chinese–Western Dialogue and Cultural Exchange

Jean-Paul Wiest

Introduction

To commemorate the beginning of the third millennium, the Chinese government built a monument shaped like a sundial. Inside, it created a long fresco celebrating individuals who have made significant contributions to the progress of civilization during the several thousand years of Chinese history. In this impressive succession of important people only two Westerners are represented: Marco Polo (1254-1324), the man who made China known to the West, and Matteo Ricci [Li Madou 利瑪竇] (1552–1610), the man who made the West known to China. Ricci is mentioned in the fresco as the promoter of cultural exchanges. With him, shown using a telescope, are two Chinese of the late Ming dynasty: Li Shizhen (李時珍), renowned for his medical discoveries, and Wang Yangming (王陽明), the famous Confucian philosopher who liberated Chinese Confucianism from its rigid scholasticism.

In this year celebrating the 400th anniversary of the death of Matteo Ricci in Beijing[35], I consider it appropriate to reflect on the person the Chinese government has deemed the symbol of the golden age of Sino-Western relations, representing peaceful interaction between China and the West on an equal footing. Why and how were Ricci and the Jesuits who succeeded him

[35] Editor's note: This article was written in 2010.

at the court successful in gaining the confidence and respect of the emperor and many Confucian scholars? Why were they able to enter into a dialogue and exchange among equals that still remains a viable and exemplary model for our times?

Ricci's Training and Formation

Matteo Ricci was born in 1552 in the small town of Macerata, in the Marche region of Italy near the Adriatic Sea. At the age of 17, he journeyed to Rome to study law, and two years later entered the Society of Jesus (the Jesuits) at the Roman College, where he made his novitiate and studied philosophy and theology. While there, he also received training in music, mathematics, cartography, cosmology, and astronomy. One of his teachers was none other than the renowned Jesuit Father Christopher Clavius, a friend of Johannes Kepler and Galileo Galilei[36].

[36] Criveller, G. (2009). The background of Matteo Ricci: The shaping of his intellectual and scientific endowment. In *Chinese Cross Currents*, Volume 6, pp. 72–93

In 1577, Ricci's superiors granted his request to be sent to the missions in the Far East. After arriving in Goa, the capital of the Portuguese Indies, he worked there and at Cochin as a missionary until the spring of 1582. That year, Father Alessandro Valignano [Fan Li'an 范安], who earlier welcomed Matteo to the novitiate of the Society of Jesus at Sant' Andrea al Quirinale in Rome, who now was in charge of all the Jesuit missions in the Far East, summoned him to Macao to prepare to enter China.

At that time, Western missionaries believed in the superiority of European culture and brought along their own cultural patterns, which they imposed on people they considered uncivilized. This attitude, unfortunately, endured among many until the middle of the twentieth century. During the sixteenth century, however, a few individual missionaries, such as Bartolome de las Casas in South America, had already acknowledged the richness of local cultures. In Japan and China also, some experienced a genuine conversion of the mind. Impressed by the achievements they observed in Japanese and Chinese literature, politics, and philosophy, they decided to make this culture the foundation of their missionary project. Valignano was the one who masterminded this new approach, which was based on the concept of a multipolar world whose center was no longer

Europe. He, in fact, wrote the first comparative study of China, Japan, and India[37]. The treatise provides interesting insights into the Jesuits' perception of Asian religions, societies, political systems, and everyday life.

Another of Valignano's outstanding accomplishments, beginning with his appointment as Visitor in 1573, was to assert his spiritual authority above the political control of the Portuguese Padroado and the Spanish Patronato and, by the same process to achieve a measure of independence for the Jesuits in China. From the start, he insisted on recruiting missionaries not deeply affected by the conquistador understanding of Christianity and the world. He knew that most young Italians trained in the Roman College of the Society of Jesus, the future Gregorian University, were free from this infection, were imbued with the ideas of the Italian Renaissance, and were intellectually well prepared.

As a result, Ricci and many of the early China Jesuits handpicked to pioneer Valignano's new model for the Church's mission in Asia were Italians. These were a distinct group of people raised and nurtured in what Andrew Ross described as "the cultural golden age of a specifically Catholic humanism." According to the new paradigm, Europe was no more the exclusive model for civilization and Christianity. It shed its Western garb and be clothed, equally well in Chinese style.

Valignano required that all Jesuits assigned to China know the language before he would let them enter the country. Upon arriving in Macao in August 1582, Matteo Ricci was therefore assigned a Chinese tutor who used the Four Books to teach him the language. A year later, Ricci and his fellow Jesuit Michele Ruggieri [Luo Mingjian 羅明堅] at the invitation of Wang Pan (王泮), the prefect of Zhaoqing, then the administrative capital of the province of Guangdong, took residence in that city. Hence began the amazing story of Matteo Ricci in China that ended with his death in Beijing in 1610.

Matteo Ricci's Relevance for Today's World

Clearly, if Valignano was the one who taught his young Jesuits to think outside the square of European culture and envisioned

[37] Wicki, J. (Ed.) (1944). *Historia del principio y progresso de la Companía de Jesús en las Indias Orientales, 1542-1564 (History of the Commencement and Development of the Society of Jesus in the East Indies)*, Rome. Institutum Historicum S.I

the new missionary model, Ricci became the one who applied it to the Chinese context. He successfully lived a completely fresh approach for the West to engage with China. In the pursuit of this goal, Ricci had at his disposal not only his training as a Jesuit, but also an impressive array of physical and intellectual attributes. He was impressive in physical appearance with blue eyes and a voice like a bell; he was endowed with a facility in foreign languages and a photographic memory; and he was keen in his ability to grasp the essentials of Chinese culture and to discern the means of entry into a sophisticated culture like that of China.

Confronted with critical challenges and dilemmas in human society, many have begun to realize that the most effective solution lies in the recognition of the diversity of world cultures, and the conducting of a continuous dialogue between different civilizations, to promote mutual understanding and trust among countries. Some 400 years ago Matteo Ricci had already adopted such a program: while in China he displayed a profound respect for the diversity of cultures, promoted mutual understanding, and was a master of dialogue on an equal footing. From a Chinese viewpoint, the Italian missionary's attitude and behavior might, however, sound more like a distant echo of Confucius. Long before Ricci stepped foot in the country, China's great thinker and educator advocated "harmony as the most precious thing" and stressed that "one could always learn from others," thus affirming that "harmony" could coexist with "diversity."

It is also important to realize that to a large extent Ricci's way of life was as much, if not more, the "result of [his] reaction to what China was and who the Chinese were" than the "proactive and creative elaboration" of "a conscious and well-defined policy conceived by Valignano[38]." In other words, Ricci became who he became because his being in China and his encounters with a number of Confucian scholars encouraged him, actively as well as passively, to rethink and reshape his identity.

[38] Standaert, N. (2010, May). Matteo Ricci: Shaped by the Chinese. In *Thinking Faith: The Online Journal of the British Jesuits*

Ricci's Respect for the Diversity of Cultures

Ricci's journey into China is therefore a journey into the minds and hearts, language and culture, symbols and sensibility of those be came into contact with. This way of life accounts for, in great part, the fascination with his achievements that extends, well beyond Church circles. He became thoroughly familiar with the long history of this rich culture, its classics, and its philosophy.

In 1594, he translated extensive parts of The Four Books into Latin and developed the first system for Romanizing Chinese. He tested the effectiveness of his work as a teaching material on newly arrived European Jesuits. For this accomplishment allowing two different cultures to communicate with each other on the basis of the Confucian classics, Ricci should be considered the founder of Western Sinology[39,40].

Ricci set also changed standard traditional European map-making when in his world maps he placed Asia and the Pacific Ocean, instead of Europe, in the central position. This work is one of his many accomplishments that show his thoughtfulness and great admiration for the empire that called itself the "Middle Kingdom." One of his commentaries, written on one map just south of the Tropic of Capricorn, declares: "I am filled with admiration for the great Chinese Empire where I am treated with friendly hospitality far above what I deserve[41]."

[39] Regrettably, Ricci's translation has been lost, although a summary based on Ricci's translation has been preserved.

[40] D'Arelli, F. (Ed.) (1998a). *Dalla tradizione storiografica alle nuove ricerche'*. Rome: Istituto Italiano per l'Africa e l'Oriente

[41] A rare copy of this map is on permanent display at the James Ford Bell Library of the University of Minnesota, USA.

When his China journal was taken to Europe and published in Latin by Nicholas Trigault[42] [Jin Nige 金尼閣], it confirmed that the kingdom of Cathay Marco Polo wrote about was indeed China, and it also reported many miscellaneous details, such as the use of chopsticks[43]. In fact, Ricci informed Europe about the identification of Cathay as China as early as 1607[44]. But most important, the journal was the first to provide Western readers with a carefully written and reasoned description of the attainments of this great civilization on the other side of the earth.

The journal also spoke of Ricci's efforts to win the good will of the Chinese people "little by little" and by living an exemplary life. As a religious man, it seemed clear to him that through the wise men of China's past God had continuously supported the development of Chinese culture and society. To his friend Xu Guangqi (徐光啟), he confided that on his way to China he had passed through many countries and had found none that could compare to China, whose Confucian and music rituals he found the most brilliant in the entire world. But when Xu asked why China remained at the mercy of natural disasters, Ricci suggested that China's scientific knowledge in some areas was still insufficient and lagging behind when compared to the West. So Xu, who had already helped Ricci in the publication of several religious books, proposed that they publish some books on European science.

Xu belonged to a group of late Ming officials and scholars who were worried about the state of the country and sought concrete ways to save it from decay. Their search was in reaction to the intuitionist movement of the Wang Yangming School that advocated that principles for moral action were to be found entirely within the mind-and-heart. They instead looked for 'solid learning' or 'concrete studies' (shixue 實學). This quest was to a large extent the reason for Xu's proposal and would over the years result in a unique interaction between many Chinese literati and Ricci, and the Jesuits who followed him.

Matteo Ricci's response to Xu's request was that they ought to translate *Euclid's Elements of Geometry* before any other scientific work because, he insisted, the understanding of Euclid's

[42] The original manuscript is in Italian and is entitled *Della entrata della Compagnia di Giesù e Christianità nella Cina*. A recent reprint of the original can be found in Quaderni Qodlibet, Milan, 2000. Nicholas Trigault's Latin translation of Ricci's journal is not always faithful and appeared first in Augsburg in 1615 under the title: *De Christiana expeditione apud Sinas sucepta ab Soc. Jesu*. In 1953. Louis Gallagher translated and commented Trigault's Latin text under the English title: *China in the Sixteenth Century: The Journals of Matteo Ricci, 1583-1610* (New York: Random House, 1953).

[43] In a letter dated Aug. 24, 1608, Matteo Ricci had already appraised his brother, Canon Anton Maria Ricci. of some of his findings: "It is now certain that China is this great kingdom that our predecessors called the Great Cathay and that the king of China is the Great Can and that the city of Pekin is Canbaluc ..."

[44] See the letter to Claudio Acquaviva dated October 18, 1607 ((D'Arelli, 2001), p. 452). See also the letters to Girolamo Costa dated March 6, 1608 ((D'Arelli, 2001), pp. 462–463) and to Claudio Acquaviva dated March 8, and August 22, 1608 ((D'Arelli, 2001), 473–474; 483–484) and to Antonio Ricci dated August 24, 1608 ((D'Arelli, 2001), pp. 505–506).

geometry was actually the key to understanding the logic of the West. At that time in China, Western logic was practically unknown. So as Ricci explained the various subject matters of the *Elements*, Xu had to expend great effort to understand what the missionary was saying and then write it out in Chinese. Shifting from a Chinese way of thinking in terms of images to Western logical thought required, indeed, a thoroughgoing revolution of the reasoning process. The two men had to go beyond the mere translation of words, sentences, and equations to make compatible two different systems of logic.

Ricci passed away after they had translated six of the thirteen books of the *Elements* (Jihe Yuanben 幾何原本). Yet, Ricci's verbal explanations and Xu Guangqi's written accounts of Euclid's *Elements* built a bridge for future generations in East-West cultural exchange that crossed the language barrier. In addition, the new Chinese terminology, which Xu Guangqi had to invent for point, curve, parallel line, acute angle, obtuse angle, etc. — concepts alien to Chinese mathematics and therefore with no words for them — soon became a standard part of Chinese mathematics.

Ricci's Promotion of Mutual Understanding

It might, at first, seem odd that the first book Ricci published in Chinese was not a tool to preach the Christian religion, but rather a small volume based on his recollection of what Greek and Latin authors had written on the subject of friendship. Entitled *On Friendship* — *Jiaoyoulun* (交友論) — this book was a way for a missionary to introduce his program to the Chinese, stating that friendship as a partnership among equals would be the root of his communication strategy[45].

Ricci wrote the book because of what China taught him. From the day he arrived he discovered the importance of true and influential friends to maintain his presence in the country. The concept of guanxi (關係), or personal relationships, has always been central to any understanding of Chinese social structures. It denotes an essential part of network-building within Chinese social life. The many difficulties encountered by Ricci and his companions in trying to establish a residence in various cities

[45] Billings, T. (2009). *On Friendship: One Hundred Maxims for a Chinese Prince.* New York: Columbia University Press

were often due to their lack of personal connections.

At the same time, Ricci's decision to write the *Jiaoyoulun* was also likely influenced by his discussions with late Ming scholars for whom the word "friendship" had become something of a code word for the promotion of a Chinese society where relationships would be among equals and entered into by personal choice. The book was widely circulated and gained Ricci a measure of fame and many visitors.

For a person whose early attempts at winning converts among the common people had ended in frustration, the success of the book reinforced his decision to shift to a top-down approach by "whispering to powerbrokers[46]," rather than preaching to the masses. He determined that he would have more success through quiet consultations with scholars and officials. This decision proved to be correct. Because of his great learning and personal probity, these conversations eventually led some to inquire about his religion. By pointing out that many of his faith's main tenants could be found in the Confucian classics, Ricci was thereby able to bring several high-ranking officials to embrace Christianity[47]. He used to tell his Chinese visitors that "the law of God was in conformity with the natural light [of reason] and with what their first sages taught in their books[48]."

After the Confucius Temple in Qufu, the birthplace of Confucius, the Confucius Temple of Beijing is the second largest in all of China. Standing next to it is the Imperial College, where the civil service examinations for the highest rank of jinshi scholar took place every three years. The names of the jinshi graduates were inscribed on commemorative stone stele, which are still on display in the temple courtyard. Among the names are those of three influential scholars who Ricci and his fellow Jesuits converted to Catholicism. Commonly known by Chinese Catholics as the "three pillars," they are: Yang Tingyun (楊廷筠), who passed the examination in 1592, Li Zhizao (李之藻), who became a jinshi in 1598, and Xu Guangqi, who passed the examination in 1604 and later rose to some of the highest positions in the Ming government.

On the one hand, Ricci and his fellow Jesuits were able to reassure these three scholars, and many others who followed

[46] James T. Areddy coined the expression in his article "Whispering Preacher Set Diplomatic Course," *The Wall Street Journal*, Digital edition, August 13, 2010. 14

[47] Spence, J. (1980). *To Change China: Western Advisers in China, 1620–1960*. New York: Penguin Books

[48] (D'Elia, 1942), p. 195. This is one of the passages that was distorted by Ricci's Latin translator, Nicholas Trigault, or Trigault's German editors, by a long theological addition about 'the innate light of nature.' Gallagher, in his translation of Trigault, further distorts it by reading the 'inner light; as 'conscience', not 'reason' (*China in the Sixteenth Century*, p. 156). For more detailed information on the subject, see (Rule, 2010)

suit, that they indeed treated Chinese friends as equals, and that the Christian message they brought was respectful of China's own culture and national dignity. On the other hand, without friends like Xu Guanqxi, who was passionate in revealing to Matteo Ricci Chinese thoughts and cultural treasures, there probably wouldn't have been the Ricci I am talking about. The interaction between these two, the genial Renaissance missionary and the earnest Confucian scholar, is a fascinating chapter in the history of scientific, cultural, and spiritual encounters. I believe that this enduring friendship based on equality in partnership serves as model for meaningful relationships among individuals as well as for peaceful and fruitful interactions between China and the rest of the world.

Ricci as Pioneer of Dialogue

Ricci's most enduring legacy may be his strategy in engaging with a culture so different from his own. "He was very deter-mined in how he pursued the dialogue[49]." He responded to the curiosity of the Chinese intelligentsia about the Christian God in *The True Meaning of the Lord of Heaven* (*Tianzhu Shiyi* 天主實意)[50]. The book is therefore not conceived as a typical catechism in the form of short questions followed by short answers to be memorized by Christian neophytes. Rather, it was a work meant to dispose readers to the reception of the faith based on reason. Ricci wrote it as a dialogue between a Confucian scholar and a sage from the Occident, and as such it is "the first attempt by a Catholic scholar to use a Chinese way of thinking to introduce Christianity to Chinese intellectuals[51]." Many of the aphorisms found in the Tianzhu Shiyi have a familiar ring to them, as if they were taken out of the Analects of Confucius:

> "The virtuous person speaks little or not at all."
> "Nothing is more conducive to a better life than to examine our conscience and discover our faults."
> "The rich miser is unhappier than the poor beggar."
> "By foolishly trying to discover the future, a man incurs misfor-tune."

Because Ricci valued Chinese respect for philosophical con-

[49] Claude Haberer, chair-person of Association Ricci, in The Wall Street Journal, digital edition, 'Whispering Preacher Set Diplomatic Course,' August 13, 2010.

[50] *Tianzhu Shiyi* was known in Europe by the Latin title *De Deo Verax Disputation* (True Argumentation about God). The book was authored between 1593 and 1596 and its draft widely distributed prior to publication. Feng Yingjing 馮應京) attempted to publish the book in 1601 but failed to do so due to economic reasons. It was finally published in Beijing in 1603. The work consists of two books, eight volumes, and 174 items in dialogue form. For a publication with both Chinese text and an English translation, see (Lancashire et al., 1985).

[51] The Chinese scholar explains traditional Con-fucianism, Buddhism and Taoism in China, and the European scholar quotes the classical works of the primi-tive Confucianists to explain the doctrines of Christianity using traditional European Catholic philosophy and scholasticism(Lancashire et al., 1985)

sideration, explanation or proof of God, the nature and act of creation, the differences between the human soul and the souls of birds and animals, he discussed these topics as well as the question of the goodness of human nature. In doing so, he strove "to expound Catholic thought with the aid of China's existing cultural heritage (Lancashire et al., 1985) ." By the same token, he displayed his deep confidence in man's ability to communicate with one another in truth and mutual respect with the help of reason and the natural and acquired talents at his disposal. Throughout the book, friendship and trust are both the starting point and the fruit of the dialogue.

From a Christian perspective, Ricci's approach to non-Christians resembled in many ways that of the early Christian Church. He went to China to spread the Catholic religion, but he carefully avoided the pitfalls of cultural confrontation. Instead, he followed a policy of cultural accommodation in an effort to reconcile two disparate systems of faith and thought. In 2009, in a message sent to the bishop of Macerata, the hometown of Ricci, Pope Benedict XVI wrote: "What made his apostolate original and, we could say, prophetic, was the profound sympathy he nourished for the Chinese, for their cultures and religious traditions ... Even today, his example remains as a model of fruitful encounter between European and Chinese civilization[52]."

Just as his use of the science and instruments he brought with him from the West dazzled Chinese intellectuals, so did his mastery of the Chinese language and cultural tradition. Ricci was thus renewing with the theological tradition of the Greek Fathers, such as Clement of Alexandria, who brought the heritage of Homer and Plato to the service of Christian thought. For a while, it looked as if Ricci successors might have been bringing about a successful insertion of Christianity within the Chinese context when, a few decades after Ricci's death, the Kangxi emperor issued an edict allowing the preaching of the Christian religion in the empire. But history did not repeat itself because the popes and most of the Christian Europe of that time failed to endorse Ricci's method of cultural accommodation. It would not be until the pontificates of John Paul II and Benedict XVI that the Church authoritatively validated Ricci's method[53].

[52] Vatican Information Service (2009, May). Matteo Ricci: A model of dialogue and respect for others

[53] Editor's Note: Pope Francis has continued to hold up Ricci as a model for engagement with China. In his letter to Chinese Catholics regarding the recent Sino-Vatican agreement, the Holy Father quoted Ricci's treatise on friendship to promote the virtue of trust (Pope Francis, 2018)

Today, attempts are underway at renewing the dialogue between Christianity and China begun by Ricci 400 years ago. The Vatican has given its full support to Ricci's approach. The author of the booklet *On Friendship* is being hailed as a missionary who undertook "a farsighted work of inculturation of Christianity in China by seeking constant understanding with the wise men of that country[54]."

[54] Ibid.

Conclusion

Reflecting on Matteo Ricci's accomplishments, Wolfgang Franke, one of the leading sinologists of the twentieth century, called him rightly so "the most outstanding cultural mediator between China and the West of all times[55]." Indeed, today foreign diplomats and business people consider Matteo Ricci's methods textbook examples for negotiating in China.

[55] Goodrich, C. and C. Fang (Eds.) (1976). *Dictionary of Ming Biography (1368-1644)*, New York. Columbia University Press

Ricci's usual demeanor, far from being confrontational, placed great emphasis on harmonious relationships. He knew how to display patience, tolerance, and kindness with his visitors. His good manners, understanding and respect for the Chinese people and culture, combined with his outstanding scholarship, enabled him to adapt himself to the Chinese environment and to gain the confidence and friendship of many Chinese literati. As a result, a number of the literati were also drawn to the Christian message he brought with him.

(Editor's Note: This article was first published in the 2011 edition (Criveller, 2011, pp. 18–28).)

Fully Translated Letters

The following five letters, Quodlibet numbers 7, 10, 36, 40, and 54, were translated from the original Italian into English for the first time for the preceding edition of this publication (Criveller, 2011). The first two (7 and 10) were translated by Roberto Ribeiro, then International Director of the Beijing Center for Chinese Studies. The third letter (36) was translated by Luciano Morra and Giorgio Magistrelli. The Traduko Agency translated the remaining two letters (40 and 54) with the sponsorship of the Mexican Embassy in Italy. All editorial commentary is from the original edition.

Letter 7: To Martino de Fornari – Padua

Translated by Roberto Ribeiro

Macao, February 13, 1583

Jesus and Mary

Very Reverend Father in Christ

May the peace of the Lord always be in our souls. Amen. You might already know from the letters[56] I wrote from Malacca that I was asked to come from India to China. We arrived in August at this port after about one month at sea[57]. The Lord came visiting me with an infirmity so serious that I almost couldn't complete the trip. But later, by the grace of God, I found myself well when I reached land.

I started studying the Chinese language immediately, and I assure you that it is something very different from Greek and German. The spoken language is so ambiguous that it has many words[58] that mean more than a thousand things, and sometimes the only difference between them is being pronounced on a higher or lower pitch and in four different tones. And so, when they speak among themselves, they write what they want to say in order to understand each other, because the same monosyllables are actually written differently from each other.

And about the ideograms, one cannot believe it without seeing or trying, as I have done. There are as many ideograms as many words and things, so there are more than 70,000 of them[59], all very different and intricate. If Your Reverence wishes, I will send you a book with their explanation. All the words are only one syllable, and their writing is more like a painting, made with the use of a brush similar to our painters. They

[56] The letters Ricci refers to are no longer extant.

[57] Ricci left Goa on April 26, 1582 with Francesco Pasio and five more companions. They reached Malacca on June 14. From there, on July 3, Ricci and Pasio left for Macao, where they arrived on August 7, 1582.

[58] Monosyllables.

[59] In fact, the number of Chinese ideograms is lower, and it differs according to different dictionaries in different epochs. The largest number is recorded by the Hanyu Dazidian (漢語大字典) (Comprehensive Chinese Character Dictionary) 1986–1989, and amount to 54,678.

have the advantage that all the regions that use this writing can communicate by letters and books, although they use very diverse languages to speak, which does not happen in our language.

As a consequence, Japan, Siam[60], and China, very different and large kingdoms, with very diverse languages, can understand each other very well with this same writing, and this same writing could be useful in the entire world. And therefore this letter ag[61], which means heaven, we pronounce it cielo, in Japanese it is pronounced ten, the citizens of Siam in another different way, in Latin it is pronounced coelum, in Greek ουρανος, in Portuguese ceo, and again in various other ways according to different languages. We have to add that nouns and verbs do not have articles, cases, numbers, genders, tenses or modes. They rather have adverbs, which clarify the meaning (of their sentences) very well. The most educated among them is the one who knows more characters, and these are the ones who join the government and noble class. This is the reason why the sciences among them are not greatly cultivated, although they believe that any man that knows how to read books also knows all the knowledge contained in books. Your Reverence might remember the similar case of a confrere of ours in Florence. He doubted, with good reason, about the new student that (claimed) to know how to read all books[62]. I immediately devoted myself to the language, I put in my head a good number of its characters and I already know how to write all the characters (that I have learned)[63].

Father Ruggieri, from Naples[64], was also here with me. He is so virtuous and diligent, and so esteemed, that the prefect[65], who is a sort of vice-governor of one of the thirteen provinces of China, invited him and gave him a place to stay, from which we expect great service for God. Since the Chinese don't believe in their idols, it will be easy to persuade them of our truth if we are able to discuss it with them[66]. But until now they have kept their law that doesn't allow any foreigner in their country[67]. It seems now that the Lord wants finally to open the eyes of this great kingdom, but we don't know how this prefect, despite the law, will be able to admit foreigners[68]. If I'm not proven mistaken, I

[60] The ancient name for Thailand.

[61] The reference to "the letter ag" is obscure to this commentator.

[62] A reminiscence from the time when de Fornari was a teacher of Ricci at the Roman College.

[63] Ricci means that he is able to write all the characters that he has learned orally.

[64] Michele Ruggieri was in fact from Spinazzola, in the Italian southeast region of Puglia, then under the Kingdom of Naples, the city where Ruggieri studied.), i.e., the mayor of the city.

[65] The prefect is Chen Rui (陳瑞). Ricci defines him a tutano, i.e., dutang (都堂

[66] Ricci will radically change his opinion about the supposed easiness of converting the Chinese, as is manifest in his subsequent letters.

[67] The Ming (1368–1644) were a nationalist regime that progressively closed the country to foreign presences previously allowed by the Yuan (1271–1368), themselves not Chinese.

[68] The prefect Wang Pan (王 泮) allowed Ruggieri and Ricci to settle in China on the condition they dressed as Buddhist monks, to reduce the foreign outlook of their identity.

will go inside in about one month[69], to where he is, and I will continue to study their language and culture.

Concerning the greatness of China, it's certain that the world does not have a greater King[70], as we can see from the many parts of the world that he owns, and which are so fertile. He doesn't have lords in his land, but governors that are chosen by him, and they are held in such high esteem that they govern like gods on earth, and are treated as such both inside and outside their homes. When at home, they don't speak with any outsider. (They receive visitors) publicly, in a very big room or hall, which seems like a church. The "venerable gentlemen" (laodie)[71], as they are called, sit in front, like one sits in a chapel, with a small table with flowers, which looks like an altar. They sit on a chair and wear magnificent garments with long horse-like ears made of fabric, which is a sign of their nobility, like the red hat of the cardinals. In the middle there is a large entrance well furnished with doors, from where no one can enter or leave but him. At each side of this entrance there are two other entrances through which the others pass, and there are many armed men guarding him, who are near him according to their ranks. Other guards are outside the door. People stay on their knees when they address him, and keep a very long stone's throw away. After receiving the answer or when the visit is finished, they are forced to run when they leave. And they give such cruel punishment for little reason, as easily as our masters punish their young students, that many die.

One day we went to visit one of them. And because of the great favor and esteem that he gives to our learning, he stood and didn't allow us to be on our knees. And so he stood like this for almost half an hour while we talked about God, as he wished to know. At the end of the audience, they sealed the door so that neither he nor his relatives could speak with other people.

When he goes outside, he is carried by four grooms that change all the time, sitting on a chair over their shoulders like the Pope. His men carry with them instruments for justice and punishment, similar to those of the Romans. These include batons, sticks, needles, and chains that they always drag in a horrifying way, three or four screaming along the road as

[69] Starting February 5, 1583, Ricci received permission to visit his confreres in Zhaoqing (肇慶).

[70] This is one of the earliest examples of exaltation of the Chinese emperor in Jesuit letters. As it is known, such description of the emperor by the Jesuits will be influential in the creation of the notion of "enlightened sovereign" in seventeenth century Enlightenment.

[71] Laoye (老爺) and laodie (老爹), i.e., old father/grandfather, are unofficial titles referred to high officials.

loud as they can so that you can hear them from far away. Your Reverence can understand that everyone runs away as if they had seen the devil. People close their doors and windows and hide inside as they feel disturbed even looking at them. This is something which I would not dare to have written if I had not seen it myself. And with this severity they have this country dominated, and nobody can raise their head; and what is worse, these laodie are the sons of very poor farmers and artisans who, because of their studies, climb to this position.

They calculated here, and very imprecisely, that the king of China has every year more than a hundred million (scuds)[72] of income. But, if it seems to Your Reverence that people might believe this is a big lie, as I am almost certain some people will think, I give you license to remove this from this letter, so that it won't seem that we are trying to augment our story if you want to share it with someone else. But I must tell Your Reverence that I think this is true[73].

The Chinese are very diligent with their things, and they have [a map of] their land printed, like our [geography by] Ptolemy[74]. They also have very diligently compiled in a book all the important elements of each place, of which I made very hurriedly a summary to Fr. Visitor[75]. However, as from now on I will be able to understand better their books, I will be able to do it more diligently, if Your Reverence so wishes. I will try my best, even if I almost don't know how to write anymore as I much forgot how to speak, as you can see from this letter[76]. Then I will send you a copy, in Latin or Italian.

The Chinese are so able in their medicine that they don't even need to put iron on their teeth. They make everything with herbs and they don't use bleeding. They have books about herbs, which we have at home, very big and painted as our Dioscorides[77]. They have books about everything, printed in great number. Their printing press is much older than ours[78], but they carve their characters on very good tables. They have to prepare as many tables as the pages that the book contains, but they are so dexterous that they can carve one table faster than one of our printers can compose a folio.

They have so many gold mines that they don't use gold for

[72] In fact, Ricci did not specify to which monetary he was referring to.

[73] The remark about the truthfulness of his testimony is revealing for various reasons: Ricci realizes that he writes things that might seem unbelievable in Europe, since there was no information about Chinese culture and lifestyle; Ricci is aware that his letters are not private but will become public; Ricci comes across as a man of honesty that accurately reports things as he sees and perceives them.

[74] Claudius Ptolemy (90–168), born in Egypt and a Roman citizen belonging to Greek culture, was the most influential astronomer and geographer of his time. He set out the geocentric theory that prevailed for 1400 years. Ptolemy is also an alternative name of Ptolemy's work *Geography*.

[75] Fr. Visitor is Alessandro Valignano. Ricci's summary is no longer extant.

[76] This is of course a sort of humble overstatement. Throughout his life Ricci's kept a good mastery of Italian language, with occasional influence from Portuguese.

[77] The reference is to the five-volume encyclopedia on herbal and other medicinal substances by Pedanius Dioscorides (c. 40 – c. 90), the famous Greek physician, botanist, pharmacologist and surgeon.

[78] Ricci frankly acknowledges the earlier invention of printing by the Chinese.

their coins, but as merchandise. They buy everything using the weight in silver because they don't have money. In sum, they have an abundance of many goods.

They adore a few idols, but when they don't obtain what they ask for, they beat them fiercely, and then make peace with them again. They adore or honor the devil as such, so that he would not hurt them[79]. Therefore, they have a very limited divine cult and their priests are not well esteemed – that's why we are surprised by the attention we receive[80].

A few Spaniards arrived here. They reached China coming from the new world, or Occidental Indies (that for us are the Oriental Indies)[81]. They went through many dangers, and we got the Portuguese to allow them to come in under the condition that they will not return. Among them were many Capuchins[82], who came here to work with much fervor, and even a Father of ours[83], thinking that China had converted already. Now they are returning on a small boat. We gave them some letters, but we do not know whether they will arrive safely.

Enough, this is all I have to say. I did not want to fail in my obligation of giving consolation to Your Reverence that, for the great love that you have for me, will be happy in receiving my letter and news. I can assure you that until I die I will never cease doing this (*i.e.*, writing letters)[84]. I can't go further away, but it seems to me that the distance won't make me forget you.

We are at $22\frac{1}{2}$ of latitude north and 125 longitude, according to the most precise information. But even though according to the degrees we are closer to the West, according to ordinary navigation we are as far from one side as from the other. As a matter of fact, from here we can reach the New World in two months, and from there to here it takes less than one year. I pray Your Reverence not trust the maps of the world, because due to ignorance or disagreement between the kings of Portugal and Spain about the borders, they contain mistakes too huge, mistakes that now will be finally put to rest[85].

[79] Ricci is most probably referring to practices held at local temples filled with statues of Taoist divinities that might have seemed devilish to him. Ricci has kept all along a negative outlook to Taoist and Buddhist religions, and will chose Confucianism as his way to liaise Christianity with Chinese culture. Ricci's attitude toward Chinese religion is best summarized by the four-character sentence: buru yifo (補儒易佛), "perfect Confucianism and displace Buddhism." This expression was used by Xu Guangqi (徐光啓) in his preface of 1612 to Ricci's Tianzhu Shiyi (天主實意) (*The True Meaning of the Lord of Heaven*) of 1603, in which Ricci launched a stern attack on Buddhism, dismissing it as a parody of Christianity. In his polemics he included anti-Buddhist arguments that he had elaborated in heated disputes with Buddhist monks, including the well-known Zhuhong (株宏), who rebuked Ricci's anti-Buddhist criticism in his Tianshuo (天説) (Explanation of Heaven), 1608.

[80] He is referring most likely to Taoist priests.

[81] From 1552 (Francis Xavier dies in Shangchuan 上川) to 1583 (Ricci settles down in Zhaoqing 肇慶) at least 50 missionaries, including Augustinians, Jesuits, Dominicans and Franciscans, unsuccessfully tried to open a mission in China.

I don't have any more paper. May Your Reverence very strongly recommend me on your sacrifices. Send my best regards to Fr. Achille Gagliardi and our common friends that might be there.

Write me many times. Farewell, farewell again beloved father.

From Macao, port of China, on February 13, 1583.

D.V.R. (Of Your Reverence)
Unworthy Son,
Matteo Ricci

[82] In June 1582 a group of Franciscan missionaries again tried to enter China. In total, there were 22 Franciscans who attempted to found a mission in China prior to Ricci's missionary work.

[83] The Jesuit missionary is Alonso Sanchez, who traveled from Manila to Guangdong province twice in 1582 and 1583.

[84] However, no subsequent letters to Martino Fornari exist.

[85] Again a candid remark by Ricci which enlightens his intellectual honesty, his being extraneous to political interests of the Iberian superpowers and his genuine interest to produce reliable maps.

Letter 10: To Claudio Acquaviva – Rome

Translated by Roberto Ribeiro

Guangzhou, November 30, 1584

Jesus and Mary
Very Reverend Father in Christ
The peace of Christ

This year I decided not to write to you, Father, to save you
the trouble of reading my unimportant letters. However, since I
came to Guangdong for some matters concerning our residence
in Zhaoqing[86], my companion Father Ruggieri asked me to send
the Catechism[87] that we have composed in the Chinese language,
and by the Grace of the Lord, it is already printed and very
well received in China. In it, by means of a dialogue between
a Gentile and a Father from Europe, all the things necessary to
be a Christian are found in it. With the help of a few of their
scholars, the information is presented in good order, in good
letters and good language. We also accommodated them in order
to refute the principal religions in China. The cover page, that
is located on the back of the book, because for them, contrary
to our custom, it is the beginning, wasn't printed yet. We were
unable to have it completed before the departure by ship of Fr.
Francisco Cabral, who has come to visit us.

We also wished to translate it into Latin or into Italian but, for
the same reason, we haven't yet finished. Your Reverence will
be consoled seeing the very difficult Chinese characters that we,
with the help of Lord's Grace, have come to learn in such a short
time. We therefore hope to be helped by the holy prayers and

[86] Zhaoqing (肇慶) was
the town where the first
Jesuit permanent residence
in Mainland China was
established from 1583-1589,
the first step in Ricci's ascent
to Beijing.

[87] *Tianzhu Shilu* 天主實錄
(*The True Record of the Lord
of Heaven*), was composed
by Ruggieri with the help of
Matteo Ricci and published
in 1584. Its content is
illustrated by Ricci in this
letter.

sacrifices of Your Reverence and of the whole Society, because such an important enterprise as this one deserves as much[88].

We also send the Ten Commandments, the Our Father, and the Hail Mary in Chinese[89]. We also send a Map of the World, in our style, but with letters, measures of miles and hours and names in their style. It was the prefect of the city of Zhaoqing[90] who commanded me to do so, and he immediately ordered it to be printed.

This is not something to be shown in Europe[91] for the many mistakes it contains; in part because of me, who didn't know it was going to be printed that fast, and therefore I did not use much diligence, and in part because of those who prepared the printing. Nevertheless, I thought Your Paternity would be pleased to see it in the Chinese language. And you should know that they hold it in such esteem that the prefect keeps the print in his home. He does not want it to be for sale, but he himself donates (copies of the map) to the most important persons of China[92].

Since I have already given a full account to Fr. Provincial, Fr. Alessandro Valignano, on the progress of this mission of ours, and to avoid duplicating the account to Your Paternity, I abstain from describing it thoroughly. In synthesis, we have finished the house we had started and although very small, all the most important people come to see it, so much so that we have no rest[93].

The prefect of the city[94] who last year had favored us so much, because of his virtue and, as we believe, partly as a gift from God for the love he shows to us, was appointed this year to a much higher position than being prefect of the city. He has been appointed lingxi dao[95], (an official) that governs many cities. Besides that, he had something that he always longed for and never obtained: a daughter, and his wife is pregnant again[96].

We have experienced many tribulations, even to the point of being falsely accused of very serious things, as the devil as thought them. But the Lord freed us from all this[97].

We have converted to Christianity only three persons. Among them is a Xiucai[98], who is a person with a degree in the literati's class. He is about to go back to his hometown eager to teach

[88] All along Ricci is aware of how specifically important was the conversion of China for the propagation of the Faith in the world.

[89] *Zuchuan Tianzhu Shijie* 祖傳天主十誡 (*The Ten Commandments of the Lord of Heaven as Transmitted by the Ancestors*) were translated by Ruggieri and Ricci in Zhaoqing (肇慶) in 1584. In the same year they translated and printed the Hail Mary, the Apostles' Creed and the Lord's Prayer. It was the first printed material produced by the Jesuits in Mainland China.

[90] The prefect was Wang Pan (王泮).

[91] Ricci seems quite aware that his letters and printed material would be made public and have an impact in Europe. His concern for accuracy is a sign of his intellectual honesty.

[92] The world map was one of the principal "ambassadors" for Ricci's fame in China, making him known in central and northern China even before he was able to settle there.

and baptize all his family and many others who want to become Christians. Following the advice of Father Francisco Cabral and the fathers from Macao, we also believe this is the best way to go. We don't want to achieve anything else other than establishing our presence so that we can keep the Christians safe[99].

We have written to Fr. Provincial about the need we have for good workers and it seems he will be able to meet our needs. Concerning the language we are very advanced. I feel that I can already confess and preach[100], and I hope, with the Grace of the Lord, to achieve some good fruits through this or through these activities. For the rest, and more importantly, I must confess to Your Paternity that I feel weak and in need of your help, for the sake of the love you have showed me, I am in much danger[101] here, a place where I am, as I hope, only out of obedience. But I don't want to start another page. Your Paternity will forgive me for writing so poorly, because here I am certain that I no longer remember the Italian language[102]. Forgive also other shortcomings.

May Our Lord be always with Your Paternity to whom I recommend myself once again.

D.V.P. (Of Your Paternity)
From Guangzhou, November 30, 1584.
Your Unworthy little son in the Lord,
Matteo Ricci

[93] The house of Ricci and Ruggieri was quite comfortable and had two floors. It was considered an attraction in the city, to the point that in 1589 the new governor, Liu Jiwen (劉繼文). made it his own house, expropriating it from the Jesuits and sending them back to Macao. Ricci refused the insultingly cheap monetary compensation for the abuse, and negotiated to be sent to Shaozhou (韶州), now called Shaoguan (韶關), in northern Guangdong, where he arrived on August 26, 1589. Avoiding deportation to Macao, Ricci saved the Jesuit mission form an early failure.

[94] Ricci is still referring to Wang Pan (王泮).

[95] Supervisor of Western Regions (嶺西道).

[96] In several cases Ricci has prayed to obtain the birth of children for childless friends, as in the case of Qu Taisu (瞿太素), the son of Xu Guangqi (徐光啓), and others.

[97] The false accusations were: the trade of children; spying for the Portuguese; endangering state security; and adultery.

[98] Xiucai (秀才), which may correspond to a European 'bachelor,' was the first academic degree obtained by those who had passed the annual examination at the county level; the other two academic degrees were Juren (舉人), i.e., 'licentiate,' obtained by those who passed the provincial examination; Jinshi (進士), i. e., 'doctor,' obtained by those who passed the national examinations held every three years in the capital.

Editor's Notes about Ricci's Maps

The first edition of Ricci's very famous world map was entitled *Yudi Shanhai Quantu* 輿地山海全圖. (*Complete Map of the World's Mountains and Seas*), of which no copies are extant. Ricci produced revised editions in Nanjing in 1600, and in Beijing in 1602 (two authentic copies of this edition are still in existence, Figure 1), 1603, 1608 and 1609.

The third edition (1602), compiled in collaboration with Li Zhizao, had a new title: *Kunyu Wanguo Quantu* 坤輿萬國全圖 (*The Complete Map of the Myriad Countries in the World*, Figure 2). The quality of this edition is much superior to the previous ones.

The fourth edition was entitled Liangyi Xuan Lan 兩儀玄覽圖 (Chart Revealing the Profound Nature of the World [two forms]). Subsequently the map had a total of 16 editions.

Contrary to popular belief, Ricci neither located China at the center of his world map, nor made China disproportionately geographically larger. The central meridian in Ricci's map falls east of Japan, leaving Europe, Africa and Asia in the west and north and South America in the east.

In his *Fonti Ricciane*, Pasquale D'Elia expressed the hope that this "tenacious legend" was abandoned forever and explained how this story started. In 1651 Jesuit scholar Giovanni Battista Riccioli wrote that Ricci put China at the center of world and drew it larger than other countries, so as not to offend the Chinese. Riccioli had misinterpreted Trigault's Latin translation of Ricci's *On the Entry of the Society of Jesus and Christianity in China*. But in Ricci's writings there is no trace of anything like that (D'Elia, 1942, pp. 210–211).

[99] Obtaining stability, security and freedom for Christian communities and missionaries was Ricci's priority. Only after securing these prerequisites would it be possible to proceed with an open and direct evangelization of the general population. Ricci's ascent to Beijing was to obtain this much needed security and freedom.

[100] Throughout his mission in China, Ricci preached the gospel to catechumens and administrated the sacraments to the converts. His activities in China cannot be described as limited to scientific and literary production.

[101] Ricci might refer here to the danger of losing high spiritual and moral excellence: he was in a non-Christian country, away from the protective religious environment of his native land.

[102] As mentioned in the previous letter, this is certainly an overstatement, in which Matteo understates his qualities to his general superior.

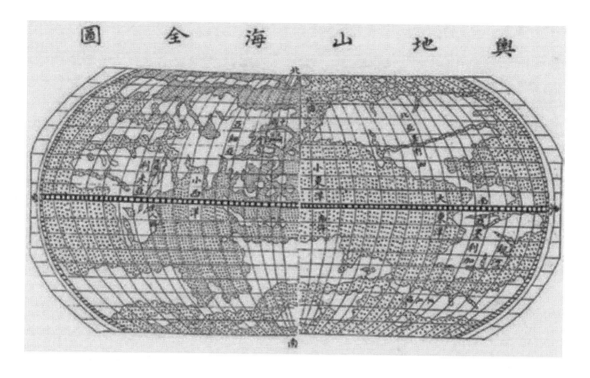

Figure 1: Yudi Shanhai
Quantu

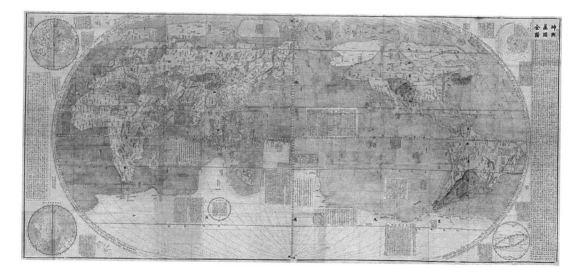

Figure 2: Kunyu Wanguo
Quantu

Letter 36: To Girolamo Costa – Rome

Translated by Luciano Morra and Giorgio Magistrelli

Nanjing, August 14, 1599

Jesus and Mary
The peace of Christ

In June, I received two letters from Your Reverence, one written at the end of '95 and the other in '96, with as much joy as they deserved; and may this be enough to express all [my joy], because, since I am in these parts, I had never reason to be so happy for letters coming from Europe and letters from my Fr. Girolamo as this time. These letters arrived to China already one year ago but I could not get them before because I was traveling[103].

Your Reverence may have already known from other letters, because I had no I time to write to Fr. General[104], how last year we tried to enter the royal city and house of this kingdom[105]. We thought we could make it but it was not possible because of the various impediments set by the enemy[106]. However, we made a lot of progress and have discovered vast areas of the country so we do not regret the difficulties, and the fruit we have harvested from them doesn't seem to be little. I have already written a very long and detailed letter about this to Father General[107] as Your Reverence suggests in your letter, so refer to it because it doesn't seem necessary to repeat the same thing to one who is so close to Father General and also because I have no time, since I spent three or four days writing it[108].

[103] The journey Ricci refers to is from Nanchang, which he left on June 25, 1598 for Nanjing and Beijing.

[104] The Superior General is Claudio Acquaviva.

[105] Matteo Ricci and Lazzaro Cattaneo resided about two months in Beijing, from September 7 to November 5, 1598.

[106] The major obstacle for Ricci's permanence in Beijing was the Korean war. See below.

[107] Literally "our father" (*pater noster*).

[108] As mentioned by previous commentators (Tacchi Venturi and Francesco D' Arelli) this sentence seems in contradiction from the one at the beginning of the paragraph, where Ricci states that he did not have time to write to the Superior General. In any case, the long and detailed letters, that cost three or four days of work, have been lost.

One month after we had left the royal city of Beijing, where I stayed two months with Father Lazzaro Cattaneo, we were caught by the winter in the city of Linqing[109], the province of Shandong. The river we were navigating iced up[110]. Since we could not stay in Beijing, we wanted to have a residence in Nanjing or nearby. I did not want to waste time waiting for the four or five months of the duration of the frost, but since we could not go all by land with all our baggage and because of other dangers, I went alone by land in the company of the two-house servants. I arrived in Nanjing two months after[111] I had left Linqing because I got sick and stopped almost one month at the home of a friend of ours[112], whom I went to visit along the way. No longer after [I arrived in Nanjing] I received the letters from India and Europe, which were at the residence [in Nanchang] in Jiangxi province. With them I received also the two letters of Your Reverence, which I read more than once, each time with greater joy and getting more news from them. I am very grateful for this and I beg Your Reverence not to stop helping me with such consolations during these few years left of my life because the sacrifices of this very difficult enterprise make me believe that I will not have a long old age[113].

It has been already four years since I received the news, only through the letters of Your Reverence, of the death of my father and my mother[114], and, being consoled by the good news that Your Reverence gave me of their departure, I have offered and am offering the due suffrages.

As for Fr. Nicola Bencivegni, besides the news received from Your Reverence, this year I have received one [letter] written by him, filled with that love he taught us, and guided us with to our present state, at our earlier and more precarious age. I will write personally to him and will do the same with Fr. Fabio de Fabii, Fr. Giovanni Paolo Navarola, and two or three others who wrote to me.

Always write to me as you do, and even more profusely, about my homeland[115], which I would never forget, also because it behaves so well and loves so much the Society of Jesus and gives her such good laborers. Sometimes I boast myself among these barbarians of being from a country where our Lord Christ, from

[109] In early December 1598.

[110] Ricci was navigating along the Grand Canal, where it is joined by the Wei River.

[111] February 6, 1599.

[112] Qu Rukui (瞿汝夔), one of the earliest and most loyal among Ricci's friends. Ricci stayed about a month at Qu's residence near Suzhou.

[113] Ricci is a good prophet here: he died 11 years later, at age of 57, of fatigue.

[114] In fact, the news was not true, as his father was still alive in 1603. Ricci must have been informed later on that his father was alive, as he wrote to him again in 1605.

[115] Ricci does not refer to Italy, not yet a nation, but rather to the region of Le Marche, then part of the Papal States.

various miles away, transported the house he and his mother had in this world. They are astonished when I tell them these and other wonders God does in the West.

I wish Brother Giovanni Battista Ferri, who went to Peru, could have come here. As Your Reverence rightly wrote in the letter, he was very apt for this enterprise in China. I would have been glad if the superiors had immediately assigned him here, but now there is no need to talk further about it because between us a great chasm has been set in place[116] and there is no exchange between these two provinces [Peru and Japan]. Besides, being so distant, the Portuguese do not allow any ship to come from there to here because it would damage their commercial activities. I have not received yet the things that Your Reverence said he had sent to me nor have I any news about them. I thank Your Reverence anyway as if I had received them all. If they are safely in the hands of ours, sooner or later they will arrive and it will be always at the right time. I also wish to send you a number of things but this year it will be even more difficult and I am not sure I can send these letters on time to meet the ship that will be leaving Guangzhou six months from now. After I have finished these few letters, I have to send a man just for this.

[116] Reference to the passage in Luke 16:26.

As for the expectation there [in Europe] to hear news concerning big conversions in China, Your Reverence must know that I and all the others who are here dream day and night about it, and for this reason we have left our country and our dear friends, have already dressed in Chinese clothes, and we do not speak, eat, drink and live in houses if not according to Chinese customs. But God does not want us to see more fruits of all our work yet, though we think that our fruit can be compared with, and even exceeds that of, other missions, which are said to do wonderful things. Our time here in China is not yet the time for reaping, not even for sowing, but for opening the woods and to fight the fierce animals and the poisonous snakes hiding in the woods. With the grace of God, others will come here in the future who will witness the conversions and the fervor of the Chinese Christians. But Your Reverence must know that our preliminary work is essential and we do deserve most of the credit for it, if we do it with due charity.

Besides that, in order that Your Reverence may also rejoice
of some of our things, China is different from other regions
and people, because the people here are wise; they are literate
and not warmongers; they are people of great talent. And currently they are dubious about their culture and superstitions[117].
Therefore, as I clearly see, it will be easy to convert a multitude
of Chinese in a very short time[118]. But on the other hand, the
Chinese had always little commerce with foreigners and never
wanted to have commercial relations with them. The Chinese
people are very fearful of foreigners, especially the king, who
is a kind of tyrant, whose ancestors usurped the kingdom by
force of arms, and is afraid that someone might take it from him.
Because of this, any large number of Christians who might join
with us would be in China the most suspicious thing that there
could be; and this is why it appears to us the most reliable fruit
and the wisest counsel that we can take is little by little to try to
gain credit with this people and to remove any suspicion, and
then to undertake their conversion. With God's grace, within
a few years we have achieved much more than many expected
because, after all, China is China, and there is no record that any
foreigner stayed here as we are. Those who came before us, who
were always just a few, were subjected to the dominion of China
or converted to their religion, or were people of low rank whom
nobody paid attention to, or somebody invited by the emperor
but not esteemed by everybody in the same way[119]. We are here
with our law and enjoy high reputation from everybody and
some, I say it for the greater glory of God, consider us among the
greatest saints who came to China, who miraculously came here
from far away. Among the Chinese there are those who understand our intention, but not everybody is willing to support us
openly, mainly out of fear[120].

Because of this, last year we tried to enter into contact with
the king, so that his subjects may not be afraid to deal with us, as
they do now; it was not possible due to the war between Japan
and Korea[121]. But the war is now over and the Japanese are
quiet, and so we hope to succeed next year.

As for this year, it was not a small thing to have the residence
in this city [Nanjing], the greatest and noblest in the whole

[117] Ricci is probably referring to the innovative philosoph-ical perspectives introduced by Wang Yangming and the sense of crisis felt in the late Ming period, which led to the collapse of the dynasty in 1644.

[118] Ricci seems here to be too optimistic. Six years later, writing from Beijing to Costa again (March 6, 1608) Ricci still holds the notion that the time for numerous conversions has not arrived yet: "...in these beginning times it is more useful to have few, but good, converts, rather than many, who may be less suited to carrying the Christian name." A similar concept was expressed on August 22, 1608, in a letter to Acquaviva: "Father, please consider that the success of our apostolate here is not to be evaluated from the number of Christians only, but from the foundation we are establishing for a very big enterprise."

[119] The sentence is not clear, however, about how someone invited by the emperor could not be respected by others.

[120] The paragraphs above are one of the most amazingly clear texts in which Ricci explains and justifies his missionary strategy, rejecting the criticism from those who pointed out that progress in China was much slower than in other missions.

of China, which is almost at the heart of the whole kingdom, and our credit and reputation grew so much in the eyes of everyone that this year we doubled all that we had in China. Although we have only established this residence, we have paved the way for many more, if we want, because many cities and provinces would like us to establish a residence. But, for the reason mentioned above, we will not open new residences before entering into a relationship with the king in order to avoid raising suspicion in the population and give the occasion to throw us out before we enter in a more stable relationship with the public authority.

[121] Ricci had the opportunity of reaching Beijing for the very first time as part of the Nanjing Minister of Rites Wang Honghui's 王弘誨 delegation. Ricci arrived in the capital on September 7, 1598, together with Lazzarc Cattaneo, Zhong Mingren and You Wenhui. However, because of the conflict with the Japanese in Korea, the atmosphere was hostile to foreigners, and Ricci's friends could not guarantee him hospitality. Two months later, Ricci had to leave the capital, and after a great deal of travelling in February 1599, he established himself in Nanjing. The Korean war, known as the Imjin War, took place from 1592 to 1598. The Sino-Korean troops repelled the Japanese invasion, which threatened to spread to the whole of China. The months Ricci spent in Beijing were the last of the bloody and six-year-long war against Japan in Korea. The situation would have been quite dramatic for the fate of China, threatened by the invasion by the Japanese. The anti-foreigner sentiment was widespread and as reported by Ricci in his account "since the Chinese cannot distinguish one foreign kingdom from the other, it seems to them that all foreigners belong to the same kingdom, or to one little different," see (D'Elia, 1949a, pp. 29–30)

Regarding what I wrote to Your Reverence, that I had started to write in Chinese, I can tell you now that I have made a lot of progress and it is unbelievable the reputation I have earned. They are crazed to see me, some because of what they have heard. Since their language is difficult to pronounce for us, I express myself better through writings and through the mere translation of whatever from our books. They confess to me that they have never heard of such science and art related information. Some want to know more about mathematics, others about moral sciences, because of all the sciences they do not have more than these two, and these are imperfect and without method. Since Your Reverence asks me something form here, I attach to this letter some sayings about friendship that I wrote four years ago in the province of Jiangxi[122] upon the request of a relative of the king, who lived there, who has the title and position of king, but without a real kingdom[123]. I will send you the Italian translation, which cannot have the same beauty [gratia] as in the Chinese language. Not only have I accommodated [accommodai][124] to them in everything, but I also changed, where it was needed, some of our philosophers' sayings and sentences and took some from our own Society. This *Amicitia* (Friendship) has earned more good reputation for me and for our Europe than what we have done[125]. While the other things give credit to mechanical and handmade things and instruments, this one gives credit, at the same time, to literature, intellect, and virtue. It is read and received by everybody with great appreciation. It has already been printed in two places[126]. I do not print it and cannot do it because, in order to print anything here, you need so many permissions from ours [superiors] that I cannot do anything, and there[127] they want to review the text in Chinese, which they do not know and cannot understand[128].

[122] *On Friendship, Jiaoyoulun* (交友論). was, with the exception of the world map, the first book that Ricci wrote in Chinese. Published towards the end of 1595 in Nanchang. the first version contained 76 maxims on friendship by Western authors. In the edition published by Feng Yingjing, 馮應京 in 1601, the number of maxims was increased to 100.

[123] Ricci wrote the book at the request of Zhu Duojie (朱多㮿), who resided in Nanchang and Prince of Jian'an 建安. It was a request that served as a literary purpose.

[124] One of the two passages where Ricci adopts the term 'accommodation,' which was how his missionary method was defined. The accommodation method, central in Jesuit missionary activity, is a concept that has its theological roots in Thomistic thought and in Erasmus of Rotterdam. It was, according to (Chinchilla and Romano, 2008), an instrument or a hermeneutical device, particularly apt to address complex religious and cultural challenges, and their doctrinal implications.

[125] The book was very well received by contemporary literati, including the celebrated anti-traditionalist thinker Li Zhi, who copied and sent it to friends all over the country. Another friend of Ricci, Su Dayong, from Jiangxi, did the same thing. In 1601, Feng Yingjing 馮應京 published an edition in which the number of maxims was increased to 100.

The other work I said I was doing is the translation of the four most important books of Chinese culture, with some annotations I added in Latin. I finished it five years ago[129]. It was so useful to ours that, with it, they understand the books with a little help of a teacher, and everyone transcribes it for himself. Fr. Valignano transcribed it for his Japan, where they study the same books, but not for Europe, where maybe it would be good to see this work. I just finished a copy for myself, but it is not possible for me to transcribe it in order to send it to you, nor have I time for it here in this life. So, I will not send it to you: be this the future care of our posterity. Currently, I have with me only one Chinese brother[130], with other young Chinese boys living in the house who will later enter our Society.

Four months ago we bought a house[131], where I receive so many important visitors that I often don't have enough time to eat. I try to eat very early in the morning because sometimes they come one after another and they force me to fast.

Fr. Lazzaro [Cattaneo] went to Guangdong to discuss some matters necessary for this enterprise with the fathers who live in Macao. He will come back within five or six months[132].

[126] After the Nanchang edition, the book was printed in Nanjing in 1599.

[127] The inquisition of the books to be published was based in Goa.

[128] This complaint about the absurdity of the process of inquisition, which caused a lengthy delay for the publication of his catechism (started in 1596 but completed only in 1603) is quite remarkable. Ricci could have shared this unconventional opinion only to a trusted friend like Costa.

[129] Ricci worked on the Latin annotated translations of the important Confucian texts known as The Four Books, 四書, when he was in Shaozhou, in northern Guangdong (now called Shaoguan), from 1589 to 1595. The Four Books are: Daxue 大學 (Great Learning), Zhongyong 中庸 (The Doctrine of the Mean), Lunyu 論語 (The Analects of Confucius), and Mengzi 孟子 (Mencius). As he states in this letter, Ricci translated The Four Books for the benefit of the newly arrived missionaries studying Chinese language and culture. He intended to send a copy to Rome, but no such text has so far been found. However, existing manuscripts by others containing Latin translations and paraphrases from The Four Books may possibly be based on Ricci's translation. For more on this complex and unsolved question see (D'Arelli, 1998a, pp. 163–175)

[130] He is You Wenhui (游文輝), Manuel Pereira.

Thanks to God I am in good health and I wish to always hear the same about Your Reverence, who is doing so well there [in Europe] that he must not envy us who are working in the East Indies.

Fr. Nicolo[133] writes that Your Reverence is already vice provincial there and I understand how busy you must be. I do not want to ask anything from Your Reverence but, if it is convenient to send something, I would be very grateful to Your Reverence if he could send me some artful and beautiful oil paintings, and other printings also artful, and those small triangular colored glasses they make in Venice, which are very cheap there, but would make highly appreciated gifts to the king and the other notables here.

I wrote to Portugal, but so far I haven't received anything. They can send from there a dozen, and if they want to be paid, we will pay them four or five times more than their value. Once everything is ready, Your Reverence write to me about these and the other things mentioned above, because, thanks to God, we do not lack here the money to pay for those things in Portugal, in India or wherever Your Reverence wishes, because it is not good to charge the province or any college where the money is taken from. In order for these items to arrive safely, Your Reverence could send them or make them be sent by Father General so that there will not be any pious interpretation or interception in India or any other place[134].

Give my very warm regards to the two brothers Alaleoni, our fellow townsmen, and to those who are there, asking them to remember me in their holy sacrifices and prayers. Do the same with Fr. Orazio Torsellino, Agostino Mazzini and all those I know. There is no need to mention them one by one because they are many. And Your Reverence, above of all, do not forget me before God, since you see in what great need I am.

D.V.R. [Of Your Reverence]
From Nanjing, Eve of the Assumption of Our Lady, 1599.
Useless Servant in Christ,
Matteo Ricci

[131] The acquisition of the house was completed only in May 24, that year. The large residence, called the "mound of Hongwu" (洪武冈) Hongwugang, was within the walls of the city, near the south gate, the imperial palace and the area reserved for ministerial and public buildings. It was sold for half of its value as no one wanted to buy it, as it was inhabited, according to local people, by spirits and ghosts.

[132] Cattaneo returned to Nanjing on March 1600, together with Diego de Pantoja and brother Zhong Mingren (鍾銘仁), *i.e.*, Sebastião Fernandes.

[133] This is the same Fr. Nicola Bencivegni, alias Serangeli, the preceptor of Matteo.

[134] The passage is not very clear. Most likely Ricci asks that gifts are sent to him in the name of the superior general so as to avoid the suspicion among the confreres that the Portuguese province is paying for them.

[P.S.] If you think they would like to see it, you can show the
Amicitia [Friendship] and the doctrine, *i.e.,* the Our Father, Hail
Mary, the Ten Commandments and the Creed, to Father General,
Fr. Fabio de Fabii, and to others.

Letter 40: To Giovanni Battista Ricci – Rome

Translated by the Traduko Agency
Sponsored by the Mexican Embassy in Italy

Beijing, May 10, 1605

Very honorable Father in Christ

May the grace and peace of Jesus Christ always be in our souls. Amen. In past years, I received your letters every year. If my letters have arrived safely, you too will have my news[135], and I can say that what they report is good as they were always about great labors in opening doors to our holy faith in this vast kingdom and the great fruit that has resulted here. So may the blessed Lord always be praised, who saw fit to use such a worthless instrument for such great work.

Things are proceeding in the same manner, and indeed are improving day by day. I find myself in this court in Beijing[136] quite close to the Tartars[137], and it appears that it is here that I shall end my days, as the king[138] shows that he wishes me to stay, and he supports and defends us, although there is not much hope that he will become a Christian. But this is not so important because through this favor many are being converted, and our other companions, 17 or 18 of the Society[139], are safe in various parts, in addition to many others who work for our people in various places, nearly 50 of them[140].

[135] This is the only letter to Matteo's father that has survived. Based on his words, he seems to have written to his father at least once a year (that would make nearly 30 letters). This is more evidence that Ricci must have written hundreds of letters that have been lost.

[136] Ricci arrived in the capital of the Ming dynasty on January 24, 1601, escorted as an ambassador, in the company of Diego de Pantoja, SJ. and the Chinese brothers Sebastião Fernandes and Manuel Pereira.

[137] The Tartars are the Manchus, who were pressing from the North and who would conquer China 40 years later.

[138] Emperor Zhu Yijun, better known by his chosen reign name of Wanli (1573-1620).

More than a thousand have already been converted to Christianity; and many others would be converted if they were not hindered by various chains which are difficult to break, the most important of which is polygamy, with the many wives which some have — at times with children — who are hard to send away; but with the grace of God, some have done it[141]. The new Christians have great devotion to (attending) Masses, sermons and other solemnities of the Church, to which they come with great frequency and from many miles away.

[139] The Jesuit missionaries present in China at the time of the letter in the Shaozhou residence included, Nicolò Longobardo, Bartolomeo Tedeschi and Jerónimo Rodrigues; in Nanchang, João Soerio, Manuel Dias and brother Pascoal Mendes, in Nanjing, João de Rocha, Pedro Ribeiro, Alfonso Vagnoni, Feliciano da Silva and the brothers You Wenhui 游文輝 (Manuel Pereira) and Huang Mingsha 黃明沙 Francisco Martins); and lastly, in Beijing, besides Ricci, there were Diego de Pantoja, Gaspar Ferreira and the brothers Zhong Mingren 鐘銘仁 (Sebastiao Fernandes), Antonio Leitao and Domingos Mendes. Moreover, China missionaries Valentim Carvalho, Lazzaro Cattaneo and Sabatino de Ursis temporarily resided at Saint Paul's college in Macao, where Carvalho was the rector.

[140] The letter reflects the timing, which coincided with one of the most successful periods of the Ricci presence in China. He was able to secure a degree of security and a certain degree of freedom for preaching. Who are the nearly 50 people working for the Jesuits? Ricci is probably referring to personnel employed at the various residences and maybe even to the close collaborators, who devoted most of their time to supporting the mission's various activities.

An old man of 72 is here who comes for all the holy days three or four miles on foot, at times in rain and snow. Another[142], who converted with all his household, though we have not yet promulgated the laws about the fasting and feasts because this is still a young Christianity, took upon himself observing (such practices) after having asked our fathers at the residence about this, and he has kept them with much integrity; and he comes to Mass on all the holy days of obligation. He had his 14-year-old son learn to serve Mass, and the first time the son served (the Mass) he came with all his household, with much solemnity. We had this man burning many images of idols and three trunks of books that contained illicit things, to which he attended before being baptized[143]. Now he confesses and receives Communion often, takes instruction and is very zealous about the spread of Christianity, and shows a desire to be a martyr.

The other day a 77-year-old catechumen came to our house with a load of bronze and wooden idols, and others painted on paper, and many books of idolatrous teachings, so that we would burn and smash them, with much rejoicing of the Christians; and he along with his wife and children and seven or eight others of his household are becoming Christians[144].

A teacher[145] with another seven or eight scholars has become a Christian. Another 13-year-old scholar also wanted to become a Christian, but the master did not want him to because he did not yet seem ready. But one day he was struck by a lightning bolt and remained unconscious for three days, in which time he saw God[146], whose image he worshiped in the schools without being a Christian, who said to him that at that time He spared his life. So with the master praying for him he returned to health and became a Christian, which is why the Christians call him Michael of the Lightning.

To another Christian, finding himself very ill, appeared the Madonna in a white robe with the Child in her arms and an old man nearby; and the Madonna said to the old man: "Make this man sweat, so that he heals." He sweated, and forthwith felt better, and now is healthier than ever.

Another Christian, falsely accused of theft and murder, and for this reason put in prison, whose adversary was much feared

[141] As it is known, the Jesuits did not compromise on this issue. The problem of concubines prevented the conversion of a number of scholars and the delay of the conversion of Qu Taixu (瞿太素) and Yang Tingyun (楊廷筠).

[142] This is Li Yingshi (李應試), also called Paolo, born in Beijing and baptized on September 21, 1602.

[143] Probably Buddhist images and books.

[144] Baptized before July 26, 1605, he was given the name Fabio, in memory of Fabio de Fabii, Ricci's teacher.

[145] This was Ignatius Dong.

[146] Anticipating dreams and visions were frequently present in the Jesuit experience and literature, and this was also so in China.

for his cunning and influence, was helped and supported by the Christians with great charity. Since the judge[147], out of fear, wanted to make an ambiguous ruling, the night before our Jesus, whose image he had seen in our house, appeared to him in a dream and asked him why he did not want to rescue a member of God's church who had been put into a tribulation. The next day he absolved the Christian and had the accuser roundly punished[148].

A Christian, Paul by name[149], a graduate in their sciences[150] who has a high office in this court[151], told me that, before becoming a Christian, he had a vision in a dream[152] that showed with great clarity the mystery of the Holy Trinity.

I do not have time to report all the things that happen here, and this little that I have written is for your consolation[153]. I am busy constantly visiting and receiving notable persons, who constantly come to ask things about our faith and our sciences. Every day I give one, two and sometimes three lessons, either to our own fathers who study Chinese letters, or to others from outside, who want to learn our sciences. On holy days I preach to the Christians and am always composing something in the Chinese language.

They have already printed some of my books, which has given us great authority in China, and beg me to have others printed. Last year the Catechism[154] was printed, which is a declaration with evidences of our faith and a confutation of the sects of China, on which I spent many years[155]; and it came out very well. Because, although the followers of the sects were angered, nevertheless many Christians were confirmed, and others were moved by this to become Christians. It was understood that since these works of ours, and especially the Catechism, arrived in Japan, they were very well accepted there, and they want them as they keep the letters of China in great esteem among themselves[156]. I am sending with this letter a version of the prayers and things of the Christian doctrine in the Chinese language[157]; and it will allow you to see the infinity of characters that one must put in one's head.

[147] Xiao Daheng (蕭大亨), at that time the presiding Minister of Justice.

[148] This event presumably occurred in late 1604.

[149] Xu Guangqi (徐光啓).

[150] He obtained the degree of jinshi (進士) on April 13, 1604.

[151] After obtaining the rank of jinshi (進士). Paul Xu was appointed custom official (guanzheng 官征). He was later appointed to the Censorate (duchayuan 督察院) of Beijing.

[152] He had this dream in Shanghai, his hometown, after the meeting with Ricci in Nanjing in March-April 1600. The dream is also narrated in the *Daxi Xitai Li Xiansheng* Xingji 大西西泰利先生行績 (*The Life of Master Ricci, Xitai from the Great West*), written by Giulio Aleni in 1630, where several paragraphs are devoted to the conversion of Paul Xu.

[153] In other letters Ricci does not go into so many details about the virtues and works of Chinese Christians. Here, Ricci is indeed reassuring his father about the good success of the mission, so that his father, originally opposed to Ricci's vocation, would not feel that his son's life was wasted.

[154] *The Tianzzhu Shiyi* 天主實意 (*The True Meaning of the Lord of Heaven*) was published in Beijing in 1603, and not 1604.

Last year much rain fell, which destroyed many houses and flooded the river[158], with great damage and many deaths; but many more died because of the famine that followed it. The king succored the people with 200,000 scudos, once each day fed all of the city's poor, and sold rice from the royal granaries at a much lower price to the poor, and I marveled at so much charity among the heathens[159].

Five of our Society are in Beijing, three priests, one Spanish, one Portuguese and one Italian, and two Chinese brothers[160]; and in addition to these there are two other companions and nine or ten in the household service.

In this house there is much activity, and in addition to dealing with local matters, those of the other three residences[161] in China write to me about various matters, as I am the eldest among us[162]. So I am quite busy in writing back to them, and I have to write to many other friends as well. From various parts of China they constantly write to me, since after 24 years[163], I have contacts in many parts of this realm.

Editor's Notes

This is of the many passages where we learn that Ricci employed a considerable amount of time in writing numerous letters to various parties in and out of China. A significant number of Ricci's letters have been lost. For example, while only two letters to Valignano have survived, their contents clearly indicate that the correspondence between the two missionaries was frequent. It is fair to assume that Ricci might have written a letter every month to Valignano, for a period of about twenty years. We already mentioned the lost letters to his father. Even more regrettable, Ricci's entire Chinese correspondence has been lost. In 1608, Ricci wrote to Superior General Claudio Acquaviva as follows:

> One of the major occupations of mine in this land is to answer, in Chinese, the letters I continuously receive from various places and from important people. People I have met long ago or even people I have never met, who nevertheless write to us because of our good reputation. (Ricci to Acquaviva, Beijing, March 8, 1608, in Ricci, Lettere, p.473).

Unfortunately, not even one of these letters (there must have been a few hundred) have surfaced so far.

[155] The composition of Ricci's most important work, initiated in 1594, was complicated by the necessity that he submit a Latin translation to the censors in Goa. The process was complicated by the necessity of providing a Latin translation to submit to the censors in Goa. Ricci has complained about the absurdity of such a process; see the letter to his friend Girolamo Costa, from Nanjing, August 14, 1599 (Ricci, Lettere, p. 364).

[156] Ricci illustrated the good reception of his Catechism in and outside China in several letters written since 1604.

[157] That is, the Tianzhu Jiaoyao 天主教要.

[158] The Bai River (白河), between Tongzhou (通州) and Beijing.

[159] As noted earlier, the description of the emperor of China as an enlightened sovereign who took care of his subjugates was instrumental in the European elaboration of the Enlightenment.

[160] They were the Italian Matteo Ricci, the Spaniard Diego de Pantoja and the Portuguese Gaspar Ferreira, plus the Chinese brothers, whose original names are unknown, Antonio Leitao and Pascoal Mendes.

[161] The residences of Shaozhou (绍州), Nanchang (南昌) and Nanjing.

[162] In fact, Ricci was the superior of the China Mission starting in 1597.

[163] Ricci reached Macao on August 7, 1582, and therefore was in China for less than 23 years.

The Map of the World which I sent[164] two years ago has been reprinted more than 10 times, and it does us much credit as it is a work never before seen in China[165].

Many write and print books about us, and this is because they have never known another kingdom than this one[166]. Now with our priests, who are valuable men, they learn many new things, and admit they cannot equal us. They are astonished by the books of images, which they think have been sculpted and cannot believe are painted[167]. They all revere them and confess that our faith is the true one.

I do not know where this letter of mine will find you, either in heaven or on earth[168]; in any event I wanted to write you. And for this reason, I recommend myself to all my relatives and friends whom I shall not cite by name as they are many, but I remember them all.

Beijing, May 10, 1605.
Your son, most devotedly in Christ
Matteo Ricci

To the very magnificent and honorable father Messer Battista Ricci of Macerata. Macerata.

[164] It must have been either the edition of 1602, *Kunyu Wanguo Quantu* 坤輿萬國全圖 (*Complete Map of the Myriad Countries in the World*), or that of 1603, *Liangyi Xuanlantu* 兩儀玄覽圖 (*Chart Revealing the Profound Nature of the World [two forms]*).

[165] In his *On the Entry of the Society of Jesus and Christianity in China*, Ricci called the map "the best and most useful work that could have been-done at this time to enable China to give credit to the things of our Holy Faith" (D'Elia, 1942, p. 208). Drawing maps of the earth was not only a tool of the missionary strategy, but involved a religious worldview: for the Jesuit cartographer, maps were not only a visual representation of geography, but a way to know and understand the work of creation. Understanding the universe with scientific accuracy meant knowing God and creation.

[166] Among those who wrote on Matteo Ricci there is the important scholar and poet Li Zhuowu (李卓吾), who wrote a poem about and dedicated to Ricci, included in *Fenshupian* 焚書篇 (*Books to be Burned*). In this passage, Ricci might refer also to the learned converts and collaborators who wrote prefaces to Ricci's books.

Editor's Notes about Ricci's Books

The books produced by Ricci prior to this letter, were the following: *Jiaoyoulun* 交友輪 (*On Friendship*). Written in Nanchang in 1595 and published the year after, was disseminated through the subsequent editions in Nanjing (1599) and in Beijing (1601, 1603); *Xiguo Jifa* 西國記法 (The Western Method of Memorization), was composed and printed in Nanchang in 1595–1596, but was not widely distributed until 1625; *Siyuan Xinglun* 四元行論 (*The Treatise on the Four Elements*), composed and published in Nanjing in 1599-1600; *Xiqin Quyi Bazhang* 西琴曲藝八章 (*Eight Songs for the Harpsichord*) were written in 1601, but were not published until 1608; *Tianzhu Shiyi* 天主實意 (*The True Meaning of the Lord of Heaven*), which we will return to later; *Ershiwu Yan* 二十五言 (*Twenty-five Sayings*), composed in Nanjing 1599-1600, this work is a translation of Epictetus's *Encheiridion* and was published in Beijing in 1605.

In 1605, Ricci also published *Tianzhu Jiaoyao* 天主教要 (*Compendium of the Doctrine of the Lord of Heaven*) in March, which contains the essential doctrines and prayers for Christian life. The booklet included the Our Father, the Hail Mary, the Ten Commandments, the Apostles' Creed, the Sign of the Cross, etc. Ricci made a clear distinction between the books on Catechism and on Christian doctrine. On this key point for the comprehension of Ricci's missionary method, see (Criveller 2009)[169].

[167] In the following year, 1606, the artist brothers Cheng Dayue (程大約) and Cheng Shifang (程士方) included four religious images provided by Ricci in their *Chengshi Moyuan* 程氏墨苑 (*The Ink Garden of the Cheng Family*).

[168] Giovanni Battista Ricci, father of Matteo, was certainly still alive in 1603.

[169] Criveller, G. (2009). The background of Matteo Ricci: The shaping of his intellectual and scientific endowment. In *Chinese Cross Currents*, Volume 6, pp. 72–93

Letter 54: To João Álvares – Rome

Translated by the Traduko Agency
Sponsored by the Mexican Embassy in Italy

Beijing, February 17, 1609

The peace of Christ

This year I received a letter from Your Reverence from December 19 of the year 1605, and was greatly surprised to learn from it that none of my letters of the previous years had reached you[170]. How this happened Your Reverence may well imagine from the many shipwrecks and losses of vessels that the Portuguese of India have suffered here and there in these calamitous years[171]. Your Reverence may be sure that it was not due to lack of respect that I did not write, as I had the obligation and such a great obligation!

[170] We have only one other letter from Ricci to Father Álvares, dated Beijing May 12, 1605. Once again we have evidence that a large number of Ricci's letters were lost.

[171] The mail between the far-off Chinese empire and Europe was mostly entrusted to the Portuguese ships that sailed from Macao to the coasts of India and then circumnavigated Africa to reach Lisbon. The "losses of vessels" in those "calamitous years" were ascribable not only to the obvious natural difficulties of such a long voyage, but also to the frequent clashes between Portuguese and Dutch or English ships. The two European powers were eager to supplant Portugal in control over the traffic between Europe and the Orient. Another way to send letters to Europe was through the "Spanish way:" from Manila to Acapulco through the Pacific Ocean; then from Veracruz through the Atlantic Ocean to the port of Cadiz; and then to Madrid.

And when I forgot, Your Reverence took care to remind me of this [obligation] with your many letters full of kindness and compassion for our travails and with so many beautiful works that you do for us and send us here so far away[172]. It seems that God wanted to make use of that piece of shared discipleship that I had with Your Reverence in Coimbra[173] to have such a necessary acquaintance for these needs of mine in the province that comes about in the distribution that is made here. Above all it pained me that Your Reverence did not yet have news of the Biblia Regia[174], which I wrote about to you, saying it had also arrived here. We suffered some distress at the gates of Beijing, as our boat overturned and this residence lost more than two hundred scudos. The Bible was lost as well but was retrieved in the middle of the river[175] by certain sailors, and we then redeemed it for three half-scudos and nothing more[176]. And although it got a little wet it is still very handsome and intact, and all day we show it to the Chinese who come to see it only for worship and its ornamentation, which puts them in awe of our holy law. The first day that we showed it to the Christians was a solemn feast day, I believe the Assumption of the Our Lady[177], on which day I said the Conventual Mass[178] with the usual solemnity. At the end of it I took the cowl and, placing the Bible in the middle of the church on a table, censed it in front of the Christians, with whom we knelt to give thanks to God for having sent to this kingdom His holy law set down in those sacred books. And these are the best ornaments of my room, where the leading figures of the court and consequently of the whole realm come to see us. With one side of the chest fitted with Chinese books and the other side with our own, which by their gold and outward splendor, well mark the difference that there is between them[179].

[172] Ricci refers here to books, scientific instruments and other gifts necessary for the Jesuit apostolate.

[173] Ricci left Italy for Portugal in May 1577, an obligatory passage for missionaries wishing to work in the lands placed under the Portuguese Padroado. In Portugal he stayed at the Jesuit college of Coimbra for about a year, where he learned Portuguese, leaving for Goa in 1578.

[174] Constant requests were made to Ricci's fellow Jesuits in Europe to send religious objects, books, and prints to Beijing as they were useful for illustrating the greatness of European civilization and Christian teachings. One of the most insistent requests was for the grandiose edition of the Polyglot Bible in Hebrew, Syriac, Latin, and Greek that was printed in Antwerp between 1569 and 1572 by Christophe Plantin with the support of king Philip II of Spain, hence the name Biblia Regia, by which it is also known.

[175] Since the times of the Sui dynasty (581-616) China boasted a widespread, efficient network of navigable canals that connected the southern regions with the northern ones. The episode narrated here by Ricci must have happened in the Grand Canal, Dayunhe (大運河) that connected Hangzhou with Beijing.

Last year I received news that Your Reverence's other kindness had also arrived in Nanchang[180], *The Works of Saint Augustine* and the *Theatrum Orbis*[181], which are so well bound that I ordered that they stay at the court of Nanjing[182], except for the *Theatrum Orbis*, which I want to keep in this center of the Chinese world, where there is greater concourse.

I should also like to extend the thanks due for so much kindness by Your Reverence, not only on my own behalf, but also that on behalf of all the others placed beneath me. But am I worthy to do this work in China as if it were mostly mine, and should I not thank Your Reverence who allows me to do a work that is really yours alone? In everything, I do all that I can for that which pertains to this mission, which I have seen brought from nothing to much by Almighty God, and together I pray Your Reverence that you continue without ever tiring because all the good that you do to us. We are very poor and have need of everything, and I promise Your Reverence that the fruit shall be such that everyone will have reason to rejoice that they helped in sowing and cultivating this field.

[176] In 1604, Gaspar Ferreira, SJ, set out from Macao to reach Ricci in Beijing, arriving in August of that year. During the journey towards the capital the boat carrying the baggage overturned, thus losing much of what it transported. However, the Bible was recovered thanks to a reward of three half scudos, *i.e.*, three giuli, a coin in use in the Papal States during the papacy of Julius II, in the first half of the sixteenth century.

[177] August 15.

[178] A Conventual Mass was the Mass celebrated for the community and the people, to distinguish from a private Mass.

[179] This is a quite interesting remark about the arrangement of Ricci's room, where he received guests. To his European interlocutors, Ricci felt compelled to confirm that he was indeed bringing Christian doctrine and culture to the Chinese.

[180] Nanchang (南昌), in Jiangxi province, is the third residence, founded in 1595, after Zhaoqing (肇慶) and Shaozhou (韶州).

I gave Father Francesco Pasio[183] a quite detailed report on things here. I think that he will report everything to Our Paternity and consequently to Your Reverence, so I will not dwell on repeating it. I am already old and weary, but healthy and strong; praise the Lord!

I had here as companion on my endeavor, for four or five years, Father Manuel Dias, who inspired this people with his zeal; and he had already bought another larger house in Nanchang, where the Christians, undismayed by the persecution of the past year[184], continue to attend the church more than ever, but now they have taken him away to put him in Macao[185]. And although I believe that it was to give greater aid to this mission, to help us to provide many of the friends he has there with alms, nevertheless he would have been happier to stay here and we wanted him here too. I do not know what Father Francesco Pasio will do.

[181] *The Theatrum Orbis Terrarum* was one of the texts frequently requested and then displayed to literati friends. A copy was included in the list of gifts donated to the emperor during the audience at the court from January 25-27, 1601. It was a collection of maps of the whole world, summing up the geographic knowledge up to that period. It was produced by the Dutch cartographer and geographer Abraham Ortelius, with the first edition of many published in 1570.

[182] Ricci arrived in Nanjing for the first time in May, 1595, but was asked to leave the town. He returned in 1598 on his way to Beijing, and finally settled there in February, 1599, returning after a two month stay in Beijing. Nanjing had been the capital of the Ming dynasty until 1420, when the capital was moved to Beijing. However, Nanjing kept the title of capital and a fictive government.

[183] Francesco Pasio, vice-provincial of China and Japan, was Ricci's superior. The long letter to Francesco Pasio was written two days earlier, on February 15, 1609. It is an important and illuminating synthesis of Ricci's own understanding of the method, problems and perspectives of the China Mission.

In his place he put Father Longobardo, who I hope will come here at the end of this year, because in the 12 years that he has been here I have never been able to see him; but now he is bound to come here to give obedience by reason of his new office[186].

Your Reverence also will be old and weary already from the many travails that the Society has in these times, but the merits will be equal to the travails and to the charity with which you help the Society, our mother, in its head and governing body.

Here the work is going better with each passing day, with various difficulties, which our people have here one time, there another. I see that we have need of many people because the field is large. It would be good to soon provide [this mission] with good and ingenious people, because our dealings are with intelligent, cultivated people.

Many times, I have asked to be sent a copperplate map of Ancient Rome[187], very suitable for showing to these people. I do not know if they fail to send it because my letters do not arrive or because there are [not] any for sale, so I turn to Your Reverence, who is the one who procures us so many good things, asking you to exercise diligence in this matter and that you address it to this court of Beijing, and any other such things that come through your hands, know that they are all very useful here.

At the end of last year it somehow came to mind that I am now the only one left of the first to enter this kingdom[188], and there was no one already here who knew the things of those first events, so it would be a good thing to write down everything in the order that they occurred, especially as I learned that the matters that I had to do with were described quite differently from how they really happened[189]. And so I have begun to make a report that I think will give great pleasure over there[190]. If, by the ships' departure for India[191], I could finish some essential part of this work, I shall send it straightaway to Rome, where Your Reverence will see it; but I doubt that my duties will allow me to do so.

[184] After settling in Nanchang (南昌) in March, 1604, Dias began intense missionary work and in 1607 decided to purchase a larger residence, partly with the idea of opening a seminary for young Chinese, but the plan was fiercely opposed by some of the local literati.

[185] In December, 1608, Dias received a new appointment as rector of the college of Macao, although he did not arrive there until May, 1609.

[186] Niccolò Longobardo was nominated superior of southern China in 1609, as his predecessor Manuel Dias had to leave for Macao. Longobardo succeeded Ricci as superior of the China mission, but they almost certainly never met.

[187] Among the maps of Rome perhaps known to Ricci are the ones drawn by Étienne Du Pérac, published in Rome by Antoine Lafréry in 1574 with the title *Urbis Romae sciographia ex antiquis monumentis accuratis delineata* and another drawn, engraved and published in Rome in 1579 by Mario Cartaro with the title Celeberrimae *urbis antiquae jidelissima topographia.*

[188] Ricci's first fellow missionaries on the great adventure in the Chinese empire were in fact no longer present: Michele Ruggieri returned to Italy in 1588 and died in Salerno in 1607; Francesco Pasio had been sent to the missions in Japan; Antonio de Almeida, Francesco Petris and Duarte de Sande died in China in 1599, 1591 and 1593, respectively.

With this letter I shall make amends, if I am not mistaken, for all the failures to write of the past years; meanwhile may Your Reverence content himself with the annual letters[192] of Father Manuel Dias, who has written them so far, and with those that are now to come from Father Longobardo.

I wrote two quite lengthy accounts of the voyage of Brother Benedetto de Goes and of his death, one sent via India and the other via Japan.

[189] Ricci has mentioned in other letters too that there were exaggerated accounts on the success of his mission, such as a great number of Chinese who were converted; or that he had easy access to the emperor, who was near to being converted.

[190] This report, later titled On the Entry of the Society of Jesus and Christianity into China, is the main source of knowledge on missionary activity in the years between the end of the sixteenth century and the first decade of the seventeenth. The history of the manuscript is well known: Ricci did not finish this work, which was completed by Nicolas Trigault, who brought the manuscript to Europe in 1614 and published it with a few modifications. The work was an extraordinary success and the first Latin edition of 1615 was followed by translations in German, Spanish, Italian and English.

[191] Letters and reports were entrusted to the Portuguese ships that sailed from Macao to India and from there around Africa to Lisbon.

[192] Each missionary residence had to send to Rome a littera annua, i.e., a yearly report on the activity carried out and on the events at each residence.

I hope Your Reverence will write to me whether over there anyone still doubts that this China is the Great Cathay, I believe that it is about time to dispel all doubts so as to be very clear. Those Moors who came in the company of Brother Benedetto should arrive here this year, and I will see if I can collect something of that which they owe him; but I do not know if I will be able to do anything as they will come here as prisoners, nor if l will be able to speak to them if not inside that palace of foreigners[193], where I am rarely able to enter. And with this I shall end this letter, commending myself and the entire Chinese Christian community to the holy sacrifices and prayers of Your Reverence.

D.V.R. (Of Your Reverence)
Beijing, February 17, 1609
Your useless servant in Christ
Matteo Ricci

To the very Reverend in Christ the Father, Father Giovanni Alvaro, assistant to the father general of the Society of Jesus in Rome. From Beijing.

[193] The ambassadors and merchants from foreign countries were obliged to reside in the "palace of foreigners" (siyiguan 四夷館), until they were received by the emperor or given permission to establish themselves in the city. Ricci himself was forced to spend a few months at the palace in 1601. It was a place he detested and used to call a castello (castle).

Editor's Notes

Since meeting with Muslims in Beijing in 1601, Ricci was convinced that Cathay, a term introduced for the first time in the West by Marco Polo, was China, and Beijing was Kambaliq, and accordingly he had informed his confreres both in India and in Europe. Ricci also stated that there were no Christians in China (before his arrival), as he had not yet made contact with the worshipers of the cross, of which he heard only in 1605. But the Jesuit community in India, based on tales of Muslim traders, continued to support the opinion that beyond the Himalayas there was a kingdom, Cathay, separate from China and inhabited by Christians. To verify this, it was decided to send Bento de Góis through Central Asia to reach Cathay. He set off from Agra (India) on October 29, 1602, and arrived in Suzhou (肅州) (today's Gansu province) on December 1605. Ricci was contacted by de Góis by letter. Ricci sent him a coadjutor brother Zhong Mingren (鍾鳴仁), who reached de Góis on March 31, 1607. The latter died only 10 days later, on April 10. The journey of de Góis confirmed once and for all that Ricci had correctly identified Cathay as China and Beijing as Kambaliq.

In the city of Suzhou (肅州) (Gansu) Muslim merchants kept Bento de Góis in a state of captivity: they stole his money and goods and destroyed his most precious travel diary. It is only thanks to Matteo Ricci that we are informed about the exceptional journey of the Jesuit Brother Bento de Góis. His incredible and heroic adventure is extensively narrated by Ricci in three chapters of his *On the Entry of the Society of Jesus* (D'Elia, 1949a, pp. 391–445). The account is based on the narration of de Góis's travelling companion, Isaac the Armenian, who managed to meet Ricci in Beijing on October 28, 1607.

Translated
Excerpts of Letters

The following excerpts are translations prepared by R. Po-chia Hsia and are reprinted with permission from *Matteo Ricci and the Catholic Mission to China: A Short History with Documents* (Hsia, 2016). The excerpts are from Quodlibet letter numbers 9, 20, 25, and 53. The short introductions are from Hsia's original publication.

Excerpts from Letter 9: To Juan Bautista Roman

September 13, 1584

Ricci's early assessment of Chinese civilization represents a mix of positive and negative views. Confident in the scientific and religious superiority of the West, Ricci was nonetheless genuinely impressed by Chinese philosophy, astronomy, engineering, and especially statecraft. Perceptively he noted the low social status of all things military in Ming China and associated it unfavorably with the unmanly culture of the literati, comparing it with the sense of honor and violence in Europe.

The knowledge of the Chinese can be seen in the invention of their characters, so graceful yet difficult, having one character for each thing, written in a most complicated and complex way...nonetheless they all study and learn these, and through them they acquire their disciplines, in which they are very learned, in medicine, in moral physics, in mathematics and in astrology. It is admirable that they can calculate very clearly and precisely the eclipses, in a manner different from ours, and how this people, who have never had any commerce with Europe, have achieved in arithmetic and in all the liberal and mechanical arts by themselves as much as we have, who had obtained this knowledge through our communication with the whole world. I only wish that Your Grace judge the Chinese through their statecraft, into which they have put all their effort and achieved such brilliance that they leave all other nations behind. If to their natural ingenuity God is to add the divine understanding of our holy Catholic faith, it would seem to me that Plato could imagine no better republic than what exists in reality in China...

China is governed by a single monarch, who succeeds by primogeniture. The present ruler Vanlie [Wanli], twenty-four years old, has governed for twelve years...The ruler governs his whole realm through magistrates, called mandarins, and they are of two categories: The first, who obtain through their own bravery and by succeeding those who first conquered the reign, are officers of war....The other category are the mandarins of letters who are much more important and are superior to those of war. All are divided into nine grades, and each grade has so many kinds of office that it will take a lot of time for us to understand...

The power and state of China is founded more on the large population, numerous cities, and good governance rather than on walls, fortifications, and the indigenous ability for war...The Chinese are little trained in war and in military arts, and they hold [soldiers] in low esteem. The military is considered one of the four lowest classes in the republic...the majority of the soldiers are malefactors from the lower classes condemned to perpetual servitude by the monarch. Only the pirates force them to bestir themselves, since they sail on two or three ships from Japan landing on the Chinese coast, seizing towns big and small in the land, putting everything to the torch and the sword without any resistance...They say the Tartars also stir them to action along the borders, but to tell the truth, whatever they write to Your Majesty about the Chinese, it cannot be said they are warriors, since both in the way and in their hearts they are more like women. If anyone shows them his teeth, they immediately humiliate themselves – yet they immediately put their foot on the neck of those who subject themselves to them. Every morning they spend two hours combing their hair and dressing, taking all the time in the world. Fleeing is not a dishonor to them, and they know neither injuries nor insults, as it is with us, having only a feminine anger...

Excerpts from Letter 20: To Claudio Acquaviva

Shaozhou, November 15, 1592, and January 15 and 17, 1593.

The years in Shaozhou were a difficult time for Ricci: two of his close companions died; he received news of his grandmother's death from Italy; and armed robbers broke into the Jesuit residence, an incident in which Ricci badly injured his foot. Nonetheless, he made important progress in evangelization and in studying Confucian texts. Most of the converts were devoted Buddhists, although Ricci's new turn to Confucianism would prefigure his later missionary strategy and his future success.

This year I made a trip with one of our brothers [Chinese Jesuit brothers from Macao] to a famous city, four or five days away, called Nanhiom [Nanxiong]... There was a Christian by the name of Giuseppe in this city, who was baptized last year [1591] in our residence, having come by himself to learn the things of salvation... Our Christian is a merchant who employs thirty to forty people in his commerce... This Christian is held in much esteem and considered holy in these parts for having a good conscience, before becoming a Christian and, in spite of his age, for fasting at all times according to the local fashion, that is never eating meat or fish or eggs or similar food, but sustaining himself on vegetables and similar food.

* * *

I noticed that most of these people whom I visited came from other provinces, and it is true what they say that in other provinces of China [other than Guangdong] there are many

more people who believe in the immortality of the soul and care
about their salvation...In these few days spent in this house
[Giuseppe's] we selected some who were most apt to receive
holy baptism and baptized ten adults and children much to our
consolation and that of Giuseppe, who said with tears of joy
in his eyes that we have come so far to sanctify his house, and
among those baptized were his son, a brother, and other relatives.
This number would have been much greater if this Christian
did not have a false opinion, namely, that to become Christian
meant leaving the world and becoming a hermit, having nothing
to do with the things of this life, just as he had done, leaving
his wife and all household affairs, paying attention only to his
salvation, intervening little in business; also being a Gentile, he
was much given to meditating in the manner of the Gentile sects
[i.e. Buddhist Chan meditation], which is not too different from
ours, always entreating me to teach him our meditations since he
is already old and does not have much time to do more good for
his soul...

* * *

The whole year we were busy in studies and I finished teaching to my companion father a course on moral philosophy in
Chinese literary texts, which are the Four Books, good moral
texts by four good philosophers. This year the father Visitor
[Alessandro Valignano] ordered me to translate into Latin in
order to help me prepare a new catechism in their language, of
which we have a great need, since the other, which was composed in the beginning [Ruggieri's *Tianzhu shilu*], has not succeeded as well as it should.

Excerpts from Letter 25: To Duarte de Sande

Nanchang, August 29, 1595

This report to Ricci's superior in Macao documents his progress
after leaving Guangdong province as well as his activities in
Nanchang, the provincial capital of Jiangxi. The visit in Ji'an is
the first description of Ricci in his new guise as a western scholar.
The reports on Nanchang focus on his socializing with the elites
and his rapidly growing reputation and success, thanks to his
books, his command of Confucian texts, and his knowledge of
mathematics and astronomy.

The following day we left Ji'an Prefecture and arrived in a
large town in its jurisdiction called Jishui District [Quiexuhien
Jishui xian 吉水縣] which could well be a city since this noble
and big place, which sits on the right bank of the river, boasts
four intendants (chayuan)...which brings great glory to this
town...in view that only one such magistrate has come from the
entire province of Guangdong...This is also the native place of
the magistrate [zhixian; Liu Wenfang] of Shaozhou District. We
found him here, having just returned a few days ago from his
ordinary visit to Beijing that all mandarins have to make at the
established time. Since Liu Wenfang was always our friend in
Shaozhou — and since he soon had to return there — I decided
to pay him a visit. As we had already decided to abandon the
name of Buddhist monks...and take the name of literati...we
have grown our beards and hair down to our ears, and at the
same time we have to wear a particular garment, which the
literati use during visits; we no longer wear the clothes we wore
before as monks. This is the first place we visited this mandarin
with beards and dressed like this...Now we are all treated

differently from before. . . and I explained to Liu Wenfang our
change in garments and that we had abandoned shaving our
heads, saying that our profession is letters and that we teach
the law of God and other things we know. Neither speaking
[Chinese] nor understanding the customs of China when we first
arrived in Zhaoqing, we were mistaken in dressing as Buddhist
monks, from whom we are totally different and opposite, since
we hold different doctrines and profess other things.

. . . In this city [Nanchang] there is a famous physician called
Wang Jilou. . . After learning this I decided to gain his friendship. . . With the friendship of the doctor and of these men [Ming
feudatory princes] my reputation began to grow in the city.

* * *

My fame spread [here]. . . Another mandarin, who is in retire-
ment, on learning that in the city there was a foreigner about
whom much was being said, and being fearful of some novelty,
went to the dutang [Supreme Commander, Lu Wan'gai] and
told him about my arrival here, asking him to look into my
background in order to find out who I was and what I was up
to. . . [The doctor] came and told me the dutang wished to meet
me the following day. I went and entered through the door. . . He
asked me different things about virtue and the doctrines we
hold, as well as mathematics and the technique for making
clocks. . . and he told me he wished me to make him a sundial
and an astrolabe.

* * *

Among the important people in this city is a great scholar,
Zhang [Huang], whom everyone calls Old Sir Zhang. He has
written almost thirty volumes of various books that have been
printed, among them some that are considered very erudite; and
he is very esteemed and considered a person of good conduct,
and a great preacher and master of the doctrine of the literati

[Confucians], which is very similar to ours because there is nothing about [Buddhist] beliefs and [it] only treats virtues and ethics in this life...

[With] Sir Zhang and his disciples I already had some debates that left them surprised, since they saw me argue so well using doctrine and arguments taken from their own books. One day, Sir Zhang — seeing himself cornered on the doctrine that I had illustrated concerning paradise and hell, which they deny, holding nothing dear but moral virtues and the good of this life — became embarrassed and said he had nothing more to say about this doctrine except for the words written by a scholar of old: "If there is paradise, good men will ascend there; if there is hell, bad people will descend there. Let's try to be good people, and not evil ones." With this sentence, our dispute came to an end for the time being.

Excerpts from Letter 53: To Francesco Pasio

February 15, 1609

In this letter, the penultimate written by Ricci, he sums up his experiences in China and offers judgment on his own work. The political situation in China was such that no one, except for the eunuchs, had access to the emperor (Wanli), not to mention the intricate and complex procedures of the bureaucracy, hence the impossibility for the Jesuits to submit a petition for regularizing their residence. On the other hand, Ricci observed from experience that many things forbidden by the law were in fact tolerated, such as the presence of Muslims and of the Jesuits. Despite many calls for the expulsion of the missionaries, they remained. After analyzing the conditions of the mission, Ricci stated eight factors that would affect Christian evangelization.

[513] Your reverence can imagine from this how it will be humanly impossible to ask for, and obtain, license to preach our law openly, because no mandarin would have wanted to present such a hitherto unheard of memorial in China. Nonetheless, some of our fathers write to me saying I need to obtain such a license. On this I say we are secure and do not require any license. We have already survived numerous petitions, submitted to the mandarins, to have us kicked out of China... I believe this not just because I understand the reasons and customs of this realm, but because we have felt the truth with our own hands. The same will be so, with the grace of God, even after we, the first ones, are dead, or this emperor should die. It seems to me that we have generated a great deal of good credit and good opinion not just among those outside of the court, but even with the mandarins of the court, and even if it is not true that the

emperor is benevolent or that he will hear us out, we should still put more fathers in different parts of China. . . until there are enough of us in China not to fear expulsion, by means of which others can enter, every year, albeit, clandestinely (as I said) like the sect of the Turks of Persia do all the time, without the Chinese noticing or able to prevent it. For I have not found the law that many say prescribes the death penalty for illegal entry; nor have we ever been threatened with, or accused under, such a law.

Ricci's Summary Reflections

The first thing is to see the miraculous progress we have made since the beginning of this mission. . . We can already count thousands of Christians, we are at the two courts and in another two important cities, and we enjoy the greatest reputation we have ever had. We converse with the leaders of the realm, and are considered not only men of great virtue but also of learning, the two qualities which are most esteemed here.

Second: since in this realm letters are highly esteemed, and consequently the sciences and rational thought [as well]. . . it will thus be easy to persuade the leaders of the realm that the things of our holy faith are confirmed with rational evidence. With the most important of the leaders agreeing with us, it will be easy to convert the rest of the people.

Third: it follows that we could more easily propagate our holy Christian religion with books that can travel everywhere without hindrance; books reach more people, more often, than we can, and can provide greater detail and precision than we can orally; we know this from experience. Because by means of the four or five books we have published up to now, our holy law and its good reputation have spread much further than before with words and other means. . . If we can put down exactly in books all the things of our holy faith, the Chinese themselves will spread our holy faith with instructions, and the converts can maintain their faith even though no priests can visit them.

Fourth: the Chinese are by nature intelligent and clever, which can be seen in their books, discourses, in the elaborate clothing

they make, and in their governance, which is the envy of all the
Orient. If we can teach them our science, they would not only
succeed in being eminent men, but we could also easily induce
them to embrace our holy law... Until now, I have taught them
nothing except for a bit of mathematics and cosmography... and
I have often been told, by important people, that we have opened
the blind eyes of the Chinese; and they say this only after hearing my teaching on the natural science of mathematics. What
would they say if they knew about the more abstract subjects
such as physics, metaphysics, theology, and the supernatural?

Fifth: ... From the beginning, in antiquity, the Chinese have
followed the natural law more exactly than in our countries.
For one thousand and five hundred years this people was little
given over to idolatry; and the idols they have adored were not
as destructive as those adored by our Egyptians, Greeks, and
Romans, but rather figures that they thought were virtuous and
did good works. As a matter of fact, the books of the literati,
which are the most ancient and most authoritative, describe no
worship except for that of heaven and earth and its lord. And,
having examined well all these books, we find in them little than
runs contrary to the light of reason and much in conformity —
their natural philosophers second to none — and we can hope
that with divine mercy, and through the grace of God's love,
many of the Chinese ancients who observed natural law were
saved.

* * *

[519] Six: the peace in which this realm has maintained itself
for hundreds of years would be useful for preserving the lives
of Christians ... and if this peace has lasted until now without
the Christian law that has pacified so many discordant ancient
realms, how will it be after the introduction of the law of union
and of peace? I have seen how this argument has served our
Christians by improving the reputation of our law and propagat-
ing the belief that if the Chinese were Christians, there would
never be rebellions and dynastic changes, which are feared so
much.

* * *

Seven: . . . through publication of our books and our participation in their rituals, we have all gained the names of learned
and virtuous men, and I hope we will continue to be considered
so until the end. This is important, because even though there
are many learned men and theologians among us here, none
of them has achieved even a mediocre command of Chinese
letters—and knowing our own language without knowing theirs
accomplishes nothing.

* * *

Eight: I want to finish this part by talking about the support
our faith has received in the books written by the Chinese literati.
Your Reverend knows that there are three sects in this realm: the
most ancient, the literati, has always governed China; the other
two [Daoism and Buddhism] are idolatrous, in disagreement,
and are always combated by the literati. Even if the literati
sect does not speak about supernatural things, their ethics are
almost entirely in concordance with ours. Thus I began to praise
the literati in my books; doing so allowed me to use them to
confute the other sects without refuting the Confucian texts, and
interpreting places that seem contrary to our holy faith.

Appendix 1: Biographical Notes on People Mentioned

Gianni Criveller

Claudio Acquaviva (1543–1615)

Acquaviva entered the Society of Jesus in 1567 and excelled for innate wisdom and capacity of governance. He led the provinces of Naples and Rome, and in 1581, at the age of just 38, he became the General Superior of the Society. In 34 years of leadership, he strengthen the Society with the promotion of the Spiritual Exercises, missions and studies. During his time as Superior General, the Ratio Studiorum was finally published (Napoli 1599) and he promoted the practice of writing the annual letters, an indispensable historical source.

Girolamo and Giulio Alaleoni

The two brothers were born in a noble family of Macerata. Giulio entered the novitiate of St. Andrea al Quirinale in Rome on May 30, 1577; Girolamo entered the same novitiate on April 18, 1587.

João Álvares (1548–1623/25)

The Portuguese Álvares entered the Society of Jesus in 1562. In the course of his life he assumed major positions of authority, particularly in the years 1594-1608, when he was the Portuguese Assistant at the General Curia in Rome. It was in that capacity that he received various letters from Ricci.

Nicolò Bencivegni, alias Nicolò Serangeli (1532–1608)

The education of little Matteo Ricci, till he was 7-years-old, was entrusted to Nicolò Bencivegni (alias Serangeli), a priest who was born in Siena in 1532 and died in 1608. Even after Bencivegni entered the Society of Jesus in Rome in 1559, Matteo maintained close relations with his first preceptor, and the two exchanged letters even when Ricci was China, although unfortunately no letters come down to us. In his letters, Ricci often mentioned Bencivegni with great affection, and stated that from him he received the first inspiration to enter the Society of Jesus.

Francisco Cabral (1529–1609)

The Portuguese born Cabral entered the Society of Jesus in 1554, and after his studies went as missionary to Japan. He filled important official positions: superior of Japan for 12 years, rector in Macao and superior of the China mission from 1582–85. He visited his confreres in the Zhaoqing residence in early November 1584. He was then master of novices, rector of the College of São Paulo of Goa, and visitor to India, where in died.

Chen Rui (陳瑞)/ Chen Wenfeng (陳文峰)

Chen Wenfeng is the courtesy name of Chen Rui 陳瑞, who Ricci defined as a viceroy, or governor-general, of Guangdong and Guangxi. Chen was also deputy minister of war, a title that was obtained through a previous job. A native of Fujian province, Chen received the first visit of Michele Ruggieri, accompanied by an official from Macao, at his residence in Zhaoqing (肇慶) in June 1582. During that hearing, he allowed Francesco Pasio and Ruggieri to come for a second brief stay in China, in late 1582 and early 1583. At that time Ricci was already in Macao, studying the Chinese language. Ricci, who did not meet him in person, describes him as "a wise man but attached to money (D'Elia, 1942, p. 161)," a view confirmed by Chinese sources.

Lazzaro Cattaneo/ Guo Jujing (郭居靜) (1560–1640)

Born in Sarzana (La Spezia, Italy) in 1560, he entered the
novitiate in Rome in 1581, and arrived in Macao in 1593. A
companion of Ricci, Cattaneo carried out an intense activity
in Shanghai and Jiading (嘉定) (Jiangsu). Together with Xu
Guangqi he founded the Church in Shanghai and baptized the
important scholar Yang Tingyun (楊廷筠), after helping him to
overcome his difficulties with the faith (1611). Cattaneo died in
Hangzhou in 1640.

Fabio de Fabii

A Roman of noble lineage, de Fabii entered the Society of
Jesus on February 17, 1567. After being ordained a priest in June
1571, he was appointed rector and novice master, in S. Andrea
al Quirinale (Rome), which Ricci entered on August 15 the same
year. The two remained in contact all their lives. Later de Fabii
became rector of the Roman College (1603), secretary general of
the Italian province (1604–08), provincial of the Roman Province
and visitor of the provinces of Sardinia, Sicily, and Milan.

Martino de Fornari (1547–1612)

Matteo Ricci's rhetoric teacher was born in Brindisi (in the
Italian southeast region of Puglia). In April 1564, he entered the
Society of Jesus in Naples. He dedicated his life to the teaching
of moral theology in Padua, Naples and Rome, where he died in
1612. He was a professor of rhetoric at the Roman College where
Matteo Ricci was admitted to study rhetoric and philosophy in
the years 1572–74.

Bento de Góis / E Bendu (鄂本篤) (1562–1607)

Born in the Azores (Portugal), a Jesuit brother, he was charged
by the Jesuit superior in India to travel from India to China,
through Central Asia, to assist the Christian communities, which,
according to the merchants of Central Asia, still lived in that
region. He also had to verify whether Marco Polo's Cathay and
Kambaliq corresponded respectively to China and Beijing. Bento

de Góis departed from Agra (India) October 29, 1602 and arrived in Suzhou (蘇州) (in modern Gansu province) on December 22, 1605. Ricci did not personally meet de Góis, but after the two were finally able to get in contact by correspondence, Ricci sent coadjutor brother Zhong Mingren (鍾鳴仁). Zhong met de Góis on March 31, 1607, but de Góis died a few days later, on April 10.

Diego de Pantoja/ Pang Diwo (龐迪我) (1571–1617)

Born in Toledo (Spain) in 1571, de Pantoja joined the Society of Jesus in 1589 and arrived in Macao in 1597. In 1600, he was sent by Valignano to Nanjing, where he accompanied Ricci on the second and final trip to Beijing (1601). He spent his missionary life in the capital, where he baptized numerous people. De Pantoja signed the petition to obtain a place of burial for Matteo Ricci. He was the author of *Seven Victories, Qike* (七克) (1614), of the earliest texts narrating the Passion of Jesus, published posthumously in 1618 in Macao.

Manuel Dias [Senior] / Li Manno (李瑪諾) (1560–1639)

The Portuguese-born Dias was called Senior to distinguish him from another Jesuit with the same name, who was his contemporary and a missionary in China as well. He joined the Jesuits in 1575. After a period in India, he arrived in Macao in 1597 with Valignano, Diego de Pantoja and Nicolò Longobardo. He was rector of the College in Macao until 1602, then he visited Beijing, and from 1603 to 1609, he held the office of superior of the missions in southern China, that is, of the three residences of Shaozhou, Nanchang and Nanjing. He engaged in high profile conflicts with some confreres. Dias held various other offices until his death in Macao in 1639.

Fabio ? (1523–1608)

We do not know the last name of this Beijing Catholic, a man of old age, who was baptized by Matteo Ricci in 1603-1604, and was given the name of Fabio in memory of Fabio de Fabii, Ricci's novice master. Fabio died early March 1608. During the last weeks of his life and in the way he arranged the funeral, he displayed a great deal of fervor that deeply impressed Ricci.

Gaspar Ferreira/ Fei Kuiyi (費揆一) (1571–1649)

Born in Portugal in 1571, Ferreira arrived in China in 1604. He was a master of Chinese novices in Beijing and Nanjing in 1605, and then worked mainly in the residences of south China. He died at Macao in 1649.

Giovanni Battista Ferri

He was, like Ricci, from a noble Macerata family. He entered the Jesuit novitiate in Rome in 1592.

Achille Gagliardi (1537–1607)

Born in Padua, after a brilliant career at the university of his hometown, Gagliardi entered the Society of Jesus in 1559 with two younger brothers. He taught philosophy at the Roman College, theology at Padua and Milan, and directed several Jesuit houses in northern Italy. He was a zealous preacher and was held in great esteem as a theologian and spiritual guide by the archbishop of Milan, St. Charles Borromeo. He authored several books on doctrine, asceticism and mysticism: *Catechismo della fede cattolica* (Milan, 1584), *Breve compendia intorno alla perfezione cristiana* (1611), and *Commentarii in Exercitia spiritualia S.P. Ignatii de Loyala* (1882).

António Leitão (1578/81–1611)

A Chinese Jesuit brother, Leitao was born in 1578/81 in
Macao. He converted to Christianity and then joined the Society in 1603, making his novitiate in Beijing in 1605. We have
only his Portuguese name. In 1607, Ricci sent him to Kaifeng (
封) to verify the presence of ancient Christian communities. The
following year he was sent to Shaozhou (韶州); he died in 1611.

Li Yingshi (李應試) (1559–1620)

Li was born in Beijing in 1559 and from 1592 to 1597 partici-
pated in the war in Korea against Japan with the rank of general.
He was an expert in geomancy, but after he met Ricci he was
attracted by Western science and was baptized on September 21,
1602, with the name Paul. He became a very fervent Christian,
devotedly observing the days of fasting and solemnities, and
earnestly receiving the sacraments. He was so fervent that he
destroyed all his books on geomancy, practiced penances and
desired martyrdom. He wrote the preface to one of the reprint-
ings of Ricci's World Map, in which he describes the teaching
of the missionaries as similar to that of the Duke of Zhou and
Confucius. He died around 1620.

Nicolò Longobardo / Long Huamin (龍華民) (1565–1654)

Born in Caltagirone (Sicily), Nicolo joined the Society of Jesus
in 1582. He arrived in Macao in 1597, and moved immediately to
Shaozhou (韶州), where he remained until 1611. Ricci 's successor as head of the China mission, he remained in that position
until 1622. He was a missionary and a sinologist of great value,
and the author of numerous books. He continued in China until
the ripe old age of 89. The Emperor bestowed honors on him
at his funeral, celebrated in 1655. He continued Valignano and
Ricci's policy regarding liturgical inculturation, the promotion of
Chinese clergy, the independence of the Mission of China from
Macao and the scientific apostolate. With Ricci's approval he
also pursued direct evangelization of the people. Ricci personally
selected Longobardo as his successor. Longobardo differed from

Ricci on the question of God's names and on the interpretation of Confucianism.

Agostino Mazzini (1531–?)

A doctor of medicine, Mazzini began his novitiate at S. Andrea al Quirinale, Rome, on December 23, 1567. He served as minister, confessor and rector in various colleges.

Giovanni Paolo Navarola

Paolo entered the novitiate of S. Andrea al Quirinale (Rome) in December 1568, and in 1593 was appointed rector of the Roman Seminary.

Wang Pan (王泮)

The prefect of Zhaoqing (肇慶), Wang played a decisive role in the birth of Catholicism in China, authorizing the establishment of Matteo Ricci and Michele Ruggieri in that city on September 10, 1583. Born in 1539 of humble origins, Wang was a good writer, poet and calligrapher. He was renowned for his kindness and fairness, to the point that a temple was built in Zhaoqing in his honor. In 1588 he moved to Huguang (Hunan and Hubei) for a new assignment. Initially he was favorable to the missionaries and curious about the tools that Ricci had with him, especially the globe and prisms of Venice, but beginning in 1586 relations with the missionaries cooled, although they never broke down.

You Wenhui (游文輝) / Manuel Pereira (1575–1633)

Chinese Jesuit Brother You Wenhui is better known by his Portuguese name of Manuel Pereira. He was born in Macao and admitted as a lay brother in the Society on August 15, 1605 in Beijing. He was the creator of the most famous portrait of Matteo Ricci, painted in Beijing in 1610 after the death of the master, and kept at the Church of the Gesu in Rome. He later resided in Nanxiong (南雄), Guangdong.

Mendes Pascoal (1584–1640)

The brother coadjutor Mendes Pascoal was born in Macao and entered the order in 1608, after serving in Nanjing and Nanchang. In 1637 he was active in Beijing, where he apparently remained until his death.

Francesco Pasio (1554–1612)

Francesco Pasio was a classmate of Ricci and Ruggieri in the Roman College, and he departed with them for Goa, India, and from there to China, where he remained a short time from 1582 to 1583. He was then sent to Japan, where he carried out his apostolate until his death. In 1600, he was appointed vice-provincial of China and of Japan. From 1608 on he was visitor of China and Japan missions.

Ignatius Qu Rukui (瞿汝夔) (1549–?)

Ignatius Qu was one of the persons whom Ricci was most emotionally attached to, and he may have been Ricci's best Chinese friend: Ricci once referred to him as 'my old and great friend'. Qu, a character bigger than life, was baptized only after a dozen years of waiting (1605). He was very close to Ricci in many ways, and it was he who advised Ricci to wear clothes similar to that of the literati (1595). He was the son of the famous Qu Wenyi (瞿文懿) from Changshu (常熟) (Jiangsu). Ignatius Qu was a man of deep intelligence and culture, despite having only passed the first stage of the civil service examination and having never won a position of any importance. He sympathized with the Donglin (東林) reform movement and lost much of his wealth in following the practice of alchemy; in fact, he approached Ricci because he believed that Ricci practiced alchemy. The two soon established a relationship of deep friendship. Ricci and Qu shared a strong interest in science and mathematics, and they translated the first book of Euclid into Chinese. Beginning in 1593, while traveling from one place to another, Qu spoke of Ricci in various cities, facilitating his entrance to Nanchang, Nanjing and Beijing. Qu gave to his son the Christian name Matthew in honor of his mentor and friend. He also assisted Ricci in many difficult times: when he was sick; during public debates with Buddhist monks and in 1598, when Ricci had to move away from Beijing, and few were willing to give him a hand. Ricci admitted that early Jesuits could never repay him the debt of gratitude.

Giovanni Battista Ricci

Matteo's father, Giovanni Battista Ricci, was an herbal pharmacist (speziale), and a member of the civic judiciary board. Giovanni Battista married Giovanna Angiolelli, also of noble birth, and the couple had 13 children, Matteo being the first-born. One of Matteo's brothers, Antonio Maria, became canon in Macerata, and another, Orazio, filled important positions in the city government. In 1596, when Matteo was in China, Giovanni Battista became a member of the city council, a body comprised of the noblemen of the city.

For centuries, the Ricci family belonged to the nobility and was the third oldest family in Macerata. Its coat of arms portrayed a blue hedgehog (riccio) on a purple background. At the end of the seventeenth century, the family was awarded the title of Marquis of Castel Vecchio (today a locality near Monteporzio, in the same region of Le Marche).

Michele Ruggieri/ Luo Mingjian (羅明堅) (1543–1607)

Born in Spinazzola (in the Italian southeast region of Puglia), Ruggieri graduated in law in Naples. In 1572, he entered the Society of Jesus, and five years later, in November of 1577, he went to Lisbon. On March 24, 1578, with Matteo Ricci, Francesco Pasio and other confreres, he set sail for Goa (India). In 1579, he was sent to Macao, and after two very short stays in China, on September 10, 1583, he settled in Zhaoqing (肇慶) with Ricci, founding the first residence in China. In 1588, at the behest of Alessandro Valignano, Ruggieri was sent to Rome to organize the papal embassy to the Emperor Wanli in order to obtain freedom for Christian preaching. Ricci prepared a diplomatic letter in Chinese language that should have been approved and stamped by the pope. But once in Rome, the plan was postponed several times because in just two years (1590-92) five popes

succeeded to the Apostolic See. In 1597, the Superior General
Claudio Acquaviva and East Indies Visitor Alessandro Valignano
decided to abandon the project. Ruggieri did not return to China
and died in Salerno on May 11, 1607, exactly three years before
Ricci.

Alonso Sánchez (1547–1593)

The Spanish-born Sanchez joined the Jesuits in 1565 and studied theology at Alcalá de Henares. He had appointments in
Spain before being sent to Mexico in 1579, where he served as
rector of the College of San Jeronimo de la Puebla de Los Ange-
les. In 1581, together with Franciscan missionaries, he was sent
to the Philippines, where he devoted himself to evangelization
and was the first secretary of the synod held in Manila. Sanchez
was sent by the governor of the Philippines to China and in 1582
and 1583 made two trips to Macao, where he met Matteo Ricci.
He was then appointed special envoy of the Philippines and of
the Society of Jesus to Superior General Claudio Acquaviva. He
later returned to Spain, where he met with Philip II. He died
suddenly while preparing to return to the Philippines.

Orazio Torsellini (1544–1599)

Torsellini entered the Society of Jesus on August 15, 1562.
He was later professor of rhetoric at the Roman College, which
Ricci entered on September 17, 1572, for studies in rhetoric and
philosophy (1572–74).

Alessandro Valignano /Fan Li'an (范禮安) (1539–1606)

Born in Chieti in 1539, Valignano graduated in law at Padua
in 1557. After serving at the Roman Papal Curia, in 1566 he
joined the Society of Jesus and completed his training at the
Roman College. On August 15, 1571, Valignano welcomed the
19-year-old Matteo Ricci into Sant' Andrea house, the Jesuit
novitiate located on Quirinal Hill in Rome. Valignano had come
to Sant' Andrea's as a one-month replacement for the master
of novices, Fabio de Fabii. Thus, the two future founders of the

China mission met for the first time. A strong bond of mutual esteem, friendship and solidarity was formed. After his month at Sant' Andrea, Valignano was appointed rector of Macerata College, in the hometown of Matteo. In 1573, Valignano was appointed visitor of all the East Indies. He visited India and arrived in Macao in 1578. The following year, before leaving for Japan, set the stage for the creation of a mission in China through an innovative missionary policy. Alessandro Valignano and Matteo Ricci had a common vision and plan for the evangelization of China, and a human, religious and intellectual accord that is quite uncommon in modern missionary history. Their close relationship was crucial for the successful founding and developing of the Jesuit mission in China. To them we owe the definitive foundation of the Catholic Church in China. The visitor imparted all the most important provisions of the first 25 years of the Chinese mission. He provided high-quality personnel, approved the opening of five residences, and indicated the goal of establishing a residence in Beijing to Ricci. He decided to make the Chinese mission autonomous from Macao. He suggested what books should be written or translated into Chinese as an aid to the apostolate. He supported the method of adaptation, *i.e.*, studying Chinese language and culture and adopting the customs of the people.

Xiao Daheng (蕭大亨) (1562–1608)

Born in Shandong, he received a doctoral degree in 1562, and first served in Shanxi. He was then transferred to the province of Ningxia, where he was governor. Having served for nearly 30 years on the border between China and Mongolia, he wrote a treatise on the Mongolian people, translated into French in 1945. In Beijing, Xiao held various senior positions in the ministries of war and justice, and he also served as imperial censor. He later became the presiding officer of the Ministry of Justice. He was also awarded the title of crown prince instructor. He died in Beijing in 1608. His nephew, with the consent of his uncle, converted to Catholicism in 1602, taking the name of Michael.

Xu Guangqi (徐光啓) / Xu Xuanhua (徐玄扈) (1562–1633)

Xu Guangqi (徐光啓), whose courtesy name was Xu Xuanhua, was the most prominent Catholic convert in the history of China. He is also an important figure in Chinese history as a scholar, scientist and politician. He was born in Shanghai on April 24, 1562, and passed the imperial examinations in 1604. He was later admitted to the Hanlin (翰林) Academy. Xu gained his first knowledge of Christian doctrine from Lazzaro Cattaneo, but it was only after meeting Ricci in Nanjing in 1600 that he began a journey of conversion. He was the first academy graduate to receive baptism, on January 15, 1603, in Nanjing, by Joao Da Rocha, taking the Christian name of Paul. He had intensive scientific and religious cooperation with Ricci, for whom he had great admiration. In 1607, he had to return to Shanghai for the ritual three-year period of mourning following the death of his father. And so, with Lazzaro Cattaneo, he introduced the Christian faith in his hometown (1608). Xu returned to Beijing in late 1610, when Ricci was already dead, and took up the defense of Christians and missionaries in 1616, during the first anti-Catholic action in China. In 1623, he became secretary to the Ministry of Rites and collaborated with Jesuit astronomers on the correction of the Chinese calendar. In 1630, he became minister of rites. In July 1632, he was appointed grand secretary, and in the following year was made a tutor to the crown prince. Xu died in Beijing on November 10 of that year.

Appendix 2: Acknowledgements from the 2011 Edition

Roberto Ribeiro

Producing the translation of these five letters by Matteo Ricci, together with the recording of the Choir of Saint Savior Church (Beitang) in Beijing, has been a long and complicated process. It involved many partners and institutions and took about a year to complete.

The project started in April 2010, as the Beijing International Society (BIS) and The Beijing Center for Chinese Studies (TBC) joined efforts to celebrate the 400th anniversary of Matteo Ricci's death. On May 27, 2010, at the Mexican Embassy in Beijing, more than 100 people gathered to listen to excerpts of these five letters, intercalated by the songs performed by the outstanding Choir of Saint Savior Church, directed by Mr. Zhou Yongzheng (周勇正).

Once translated, we realized that these letters were destined to be published. Many friends requested copies, and without hesitation Dr. Jean-Paul Wiest, then TBC's research director, started to prepare them for printing in a booklet, which proved to be a more complicated process than expected.

First, we had to complete the translation of the five letters. We soon realized that a translation for publication required special attention, especially when we wanted to add critical notes explaining the context and difficult passages. The project was later entrusted to the excellent hands of Gianni Criveller, who in late 2010 joined TBC as the new research director. Under his supervision, this simple publication became a unique document that now finally reaches the interested reader.

The booklet has many authors. The introduction, all critical notes and the biographical sketches were prepared by Gianni Criveller, who coordinated the core of this project. Jean Paul Wiest, TBC's Research Director until 2010, wrote a commentary on the significance of Matteo Ricci today, which was originally presented at the Nishan Forum in August 2010.

The first two letters were translated by Roberto Ribeiro. The third letter was translated by Luciano Morra and partly by Giorgio Magistrelli. The fourth and fifth letters were translated by the Traduko Agency, sponsored by the Mexican Embassy in Italy.

Paul Mooney has kindly proofread the early draft. Ann Dewi Mooney has provided the layout for the booklet.

The publication includes a CD of Matteo Ricci's related music and songs by the Choir of Saint Savior Church in Beijing (Beitang), directed by Mr. Zhou Yongzheng (周勇正).

This publication has a limited circulation but we hope it will be conducive to a major project to translate and provide commentary on the complete corpus of Ricci's letters. Suggestions, collaboration and support are very much encouraged and welcomed.

Appendix 3: Images of Original Autographs

To give the reader a sense of what the original letters written by Matteo Ricci look like, we have included some scanned images of autographs of Ricci's letters. About half (26) of Ricci's original letters are held in the Archivum Romanum Societatis Iesu (ARSI) *Japonica-Sinica* collection. The images included here are a selection from three of the clearer autographs in the ARSI collection.

Figures 3 and 4 are the first page and address page of Letter 8, written to Father General Acquaviva from Macao on the same date as Letter 7 which is included in this volume. Figure 5 is of the first page of Letter 10, also to Acquaviva. The style of formal greetings at the top are typical. Figures 6, 7, and 8 are of Letter 25, from Nanjing to D. de Sande. They are a good sample of Ricci's handwriting. Figure 8 also includes a clear example of Ricci's signature.

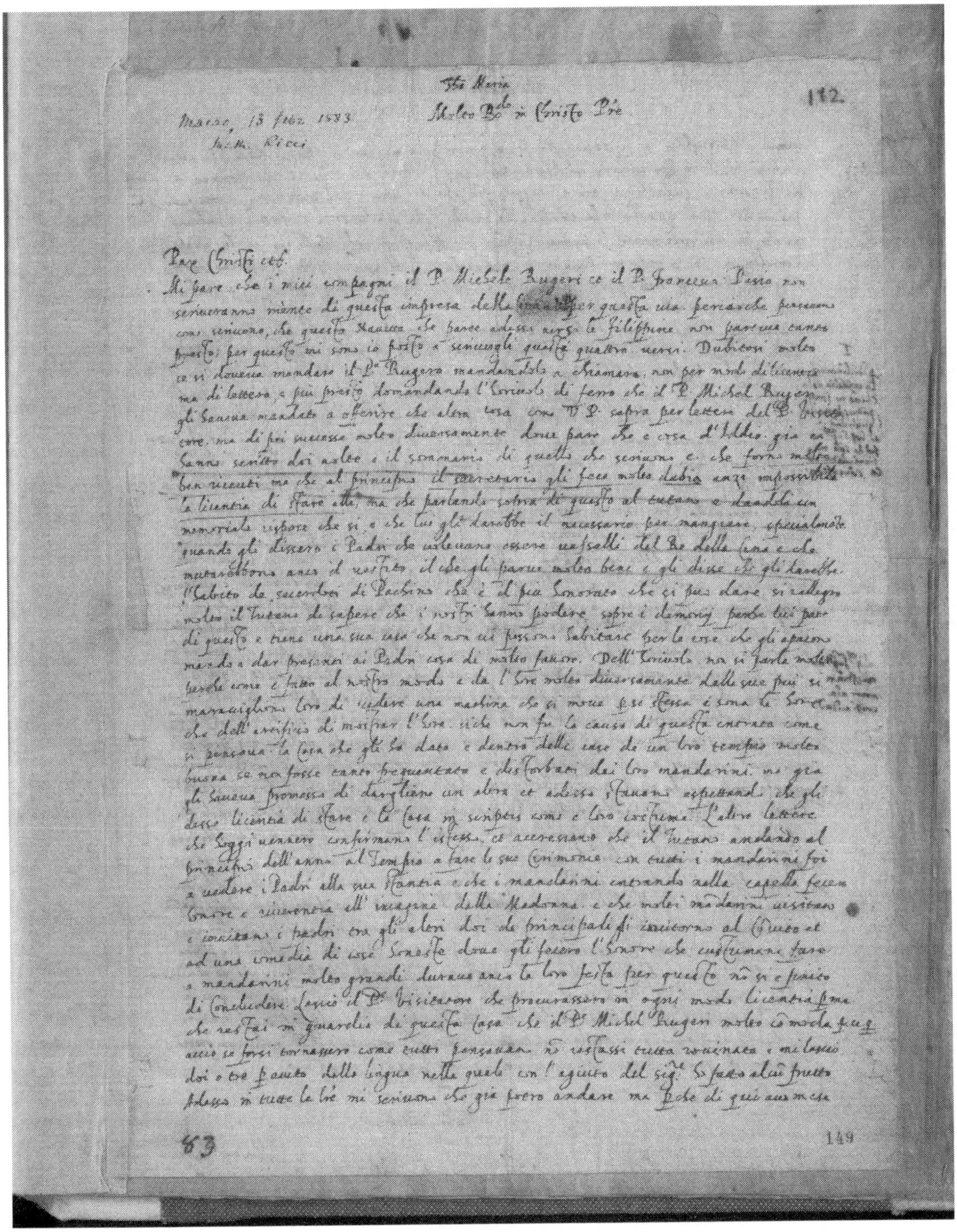
Jhs Maria
Molto Rdo in Christo Pre
182
Macao, 13 febr. 1583
Mth. Ricci
Pax Christi etc.
83
149

Figure 3: Letter 8; ARSI *Jap.Sin.* 9, 1, 149r

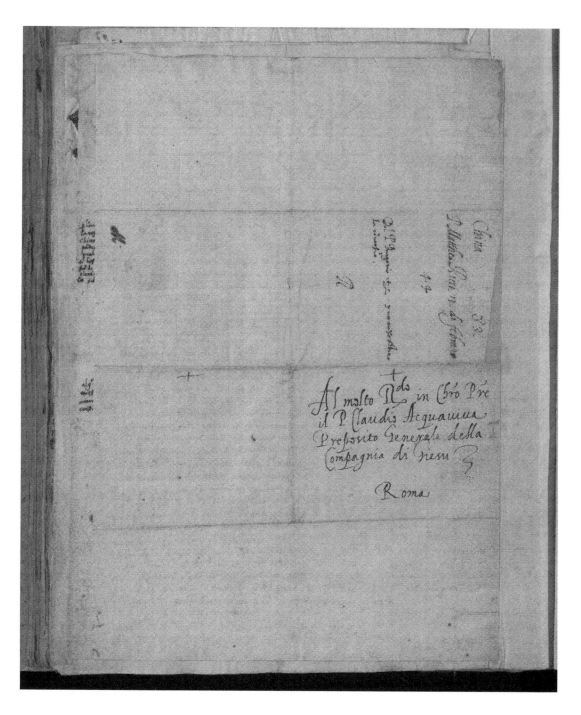

Figure 4: Letter 8; ARSI
Jap.Sin. 9, 1, 150v

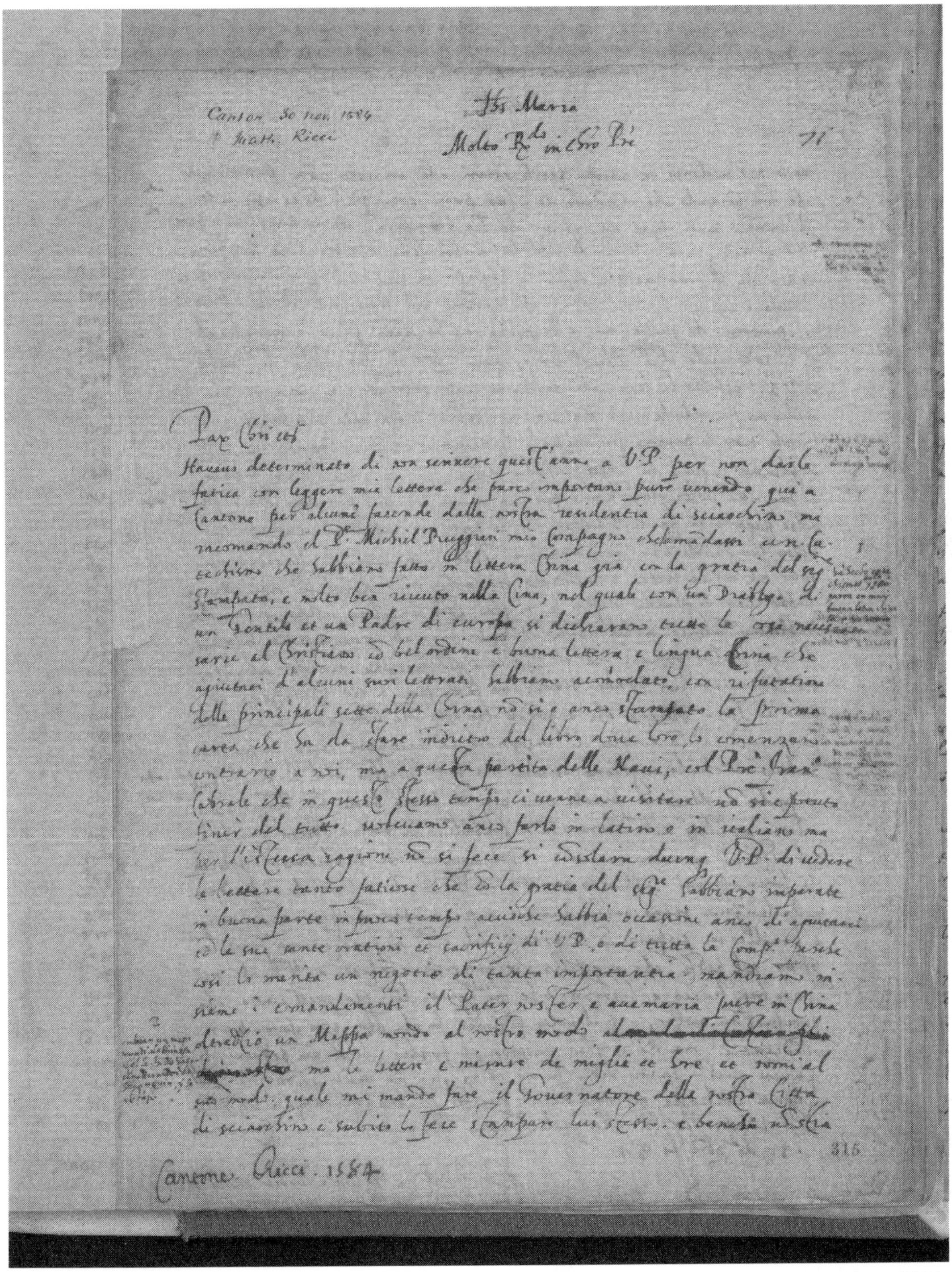

Canton 30 nov. 1584
P. Matt. Ricci

Jhs Maria
Molto R.do in Cristo P.re

71

Pax Christi
Havevo determinato di non scrivere quest'anno a V.P. per non darle
fatica con leggere mie lettere che fusse importanti pure venendo qua a
Cantone per alcune facende della nostra residentia di Sciauchino mi
raccomandò el P. Michel Ruggieri mio compagno che le mandassi un catechismo che habbiamo fatto in lettera China già con la gratia del Sig.re
stampato, e molto ben ricevuto nella Cina, nel quale con un Dialogo di
un Gentile et un Padre di Europa si dichiarano tutte le cose neces-
sarie al Christiano con bel ordine e buona lettera e lingua China che
ajutati d'alcuni suoi letterati habbiamo accomodato, con rifutatione
delle principali sette della Cina. Non si è ancora stampato la prima
carta che ha da stare indietro del libro dove loro lo cominciano
contrario a noi, ma a questa partita delle navi, col P.re Fran.co
Cabral che in questo stesso tempo ci venne a visitare non si è potuto
finir del tutto. Volevamo ancor farlo in latino e in italiano ma
per l'istessa ragione non si fece. Si contentarà dunque V.P. di vedere
le lettere tanto fatiose che con la gratia del Sig.re habbiamo imparate
in buona parte in poco tempo accioche habbia occasione ancor di ajutarci
con le sue sante orationi et sacrificij di V.P. e di tutta la Comp.a perche
così lo merita un negotio di tanta importantia. Mandiamo in-
sieme i comandamenti il Pater noster e avemaria pure in China
Ho fatto un Mappamondo al nostro modo ~~[illegible]~~
~~[illegible]~~ ma le lettere e misure de miglia et hore et nomi al
suo modo, quale mi mandò fare il Governatore della nostra Città
di Sciauchino e subito lo fece stampare lui stesso. e benche non stia

315

Cantone Ricci . 1584

Figure 5: Letter 10; ARSI *Jap.Sin.* 9, 2, 315r

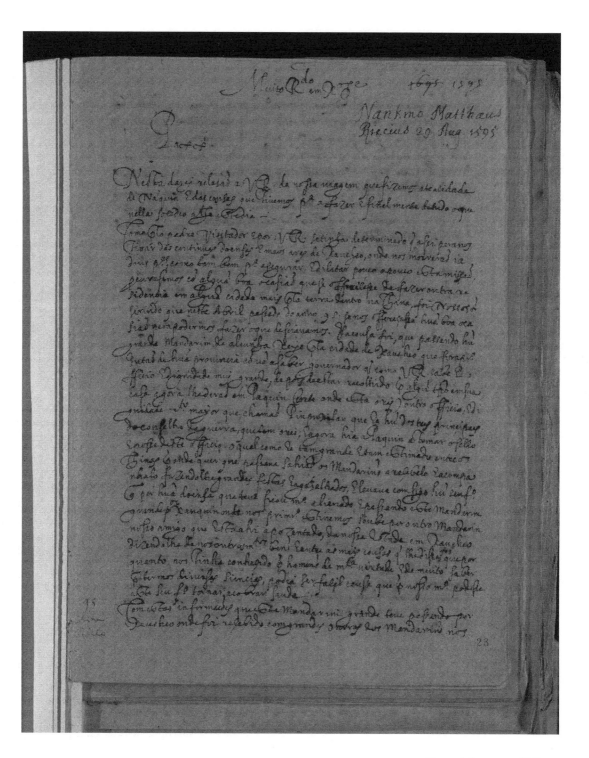

Figure 6: Letter 25; ARSI
Jap.Sin. 113, 23r

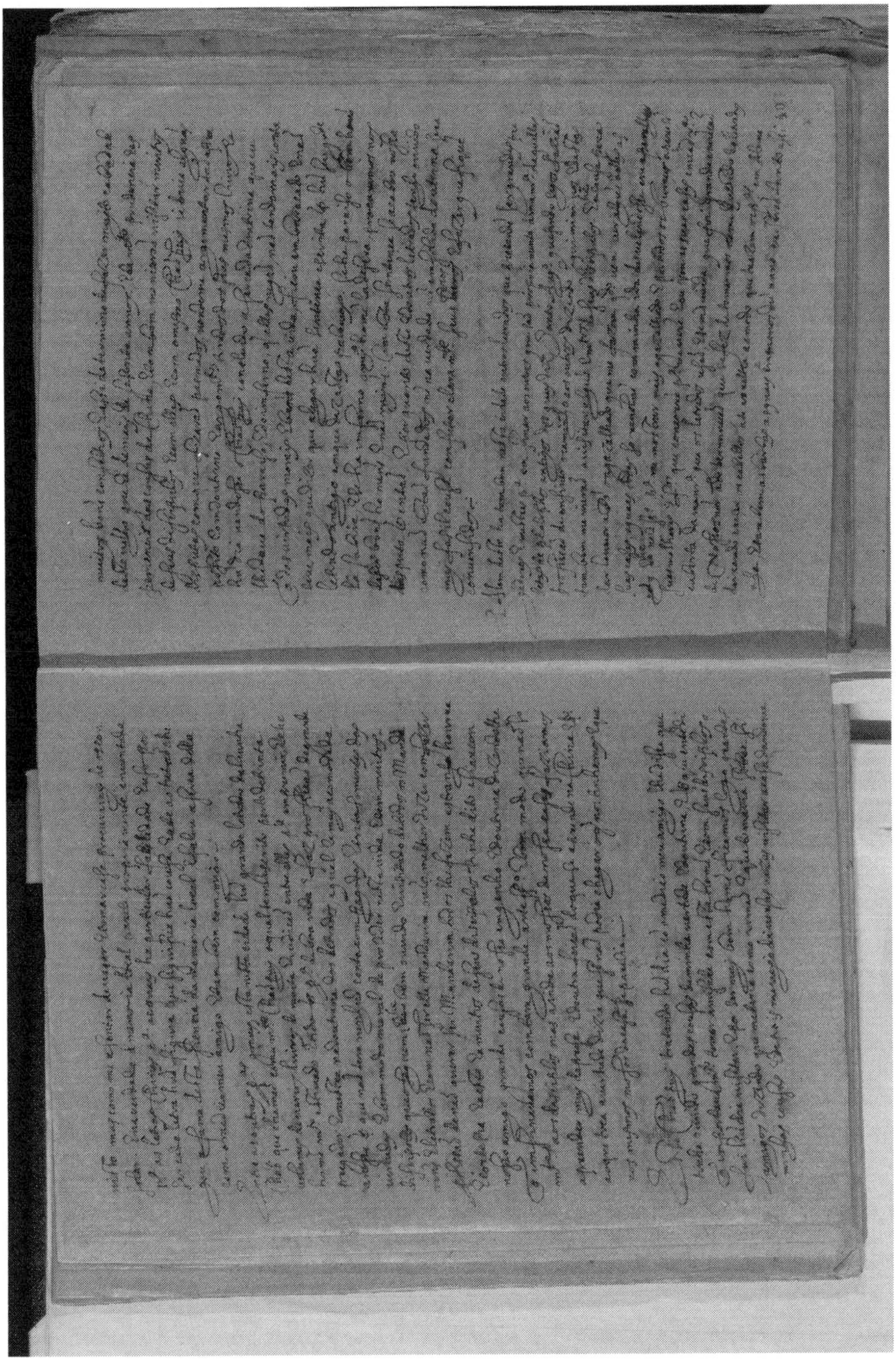

Figure 7: Letter 25; ARSI *Jap.Sin.* 113, 39v-40r

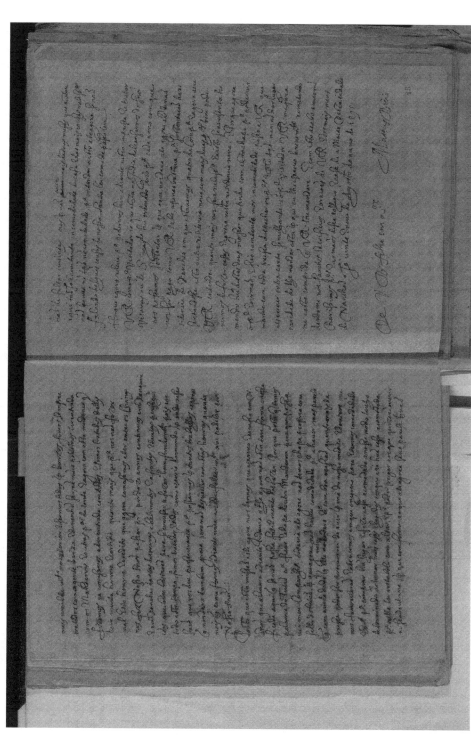

Figure 8: Letter 25; ARSI
Jap.Sin. 113, 42v-43r

About the Contributors and Editors

Contributors

Thierry Meynard, S.J., born in France in 1963, is currently professor and PhD director at the philosophy department of Sun Yat-Sen University, Guangzhou, where he teaches Western Philosophy and Latin Classics. He is the vice-director of the Archive for Introduction of Western Knowledge at Sun Yat-Sen University. In 2012-2014, he was director of The Beijing Center for Chinese Studies. He holds a PhD in Philosophy from Peking University, presenting a thesis on Liang Shuming. From 2003 to 2006, he taught philosophy at Fordham University, New York. Since 2006, he is a member of the Macau Ricci Institute. He has authored *The Jesuit Reading of Confucius* (Boston: Brill, 2015), *The Religious Philosophy of Liang Shuming* (Boston: Brill, 2011), *Confucius Sinarum Philosophus* (Rome: IHSI, 2011), and co-authored with Sher-shiueh Li, *Jesuit Chreia in Late Ming China* (Bern: Peter Lang: 2014).

Michela Fontana is the author of the award-winning biography entitled *Matteo Ricci: A Jesuit in the Ming Court*. She holds a degree in mathematics from Milan State University where she has also taught. Her accolades include the Knight Science Fellowship at MIT, the Glaxo Prize for science journalism, the Pirelli International award for the popularization of science, and the 2010 Grand Prix de la Biographie Politique. She has also written the script for the play *Matteo Ricci, a Jesuit Scientist at the Ming Court*.

Eugene Geinzer, S.J., grew up among the hills of Western Pennsylvania where his fascination with architecture first began. As a boy he would sketch the houses which conformed as best they could to the rigors of the hills. After completing high school, he decided to enter the Society of Jesus, which took him to the Amish country of Eastern Pennsylvania, the humid basins of Mobile Bay, the hard concrete of New York City, the sultry bayou of Louisiana. Fr. Geinzer taught philosophy of art, three-dimensional design and drawing at Georgetown and Loyola Chicago, but in his summer months explored Central Mexico, the Yucatan and down into Ecuador and Peru's Amazon. When the opportunity to have a sabbatical in Beijing arose, it was the opening to a new continent of surprises. Gradually, over the course of 12 years, Fr. Geinzer enhanced an array of programs that gave great joy to him and TBC's students. Currently, he is the House Manager at the East Coast Jesuit novitiate in Syracuse, NY.

Amy Yu Fu is associate professor of English at Zhejiang University City College. She received her Ph.D. in religion from the Dept. of Philosophy, Zhejiang University. From 2014 to 2016, She was a visiting scholar at Harvard University. She has translated several books in the field of religion and her commentary and translation of Dao De Jing (English) is forthcoming. Her articles have appeared in peer-reviewed journals home and abroad. She has also presented papers at conferences in China, America, Korea and Australia on comparative religion and interreligious dialogue. Her research interest includes the cultural interaction between China and the West in the seventeenth century.

Antonio De Caro is an Italian PhD student at Hong Kong Baptist University under the supervision of Prof. Lo Ping-Cheung. He is mostly interested in the history of the Society of Jesus in China as well as the interactions between Chinese and European philosophies. His current doctoral dissertation is related to Fr. Angelo Zottoli, S.J. (晁德莅, 1826-1902), a Jesuit missionary who lived in Shanghai for more than fifty years, and his cosmogonic writings.

Jean-Paul Wiest is a researcher primarily focused on the history of Sino-Western cultural and religious interactions. From 2003

to 2011, he was the Research Director of the Beijing Center
for Chinese Studies. He has published extensively in English,
French, and Chinese. His books include *Maryknoll in China: A
History, 1918-1955* (1988, 1997), The Catholic Church in Modern
China (1993), 歷史遺蹤 – 正福寺天主教墓地 [*When Stone Speaks:
Beijing Zhengfusi Cemetery*] (2007), and 述史研究方法 [*Oral History
Methods*] (2010). Dr. Wiest holds a Licentiate in Theology (1966)
from the Jesuit Faculty of Theology in Egenhoven, Belgium,
and a Ph.D. in Chinese History (1977) from the University of
Washington, U.S.A. His dissertation was on the return of MEP
missionaries to the province of Guangdong and Guangxi in the
late 1840s.

Editors

Brendan Gottschall, S.J., is a Jesuit scholastic for the Maryland
Province of the Society of Jesus and is currently a research associate at the Beijing Center for Chinese Studies. His interest
in China began with the study of the Chinese language in un-
dergraduate studies. He recently earned a Master's degree in
Philosophy from Fordham University, writing his thesis on the
just price theory of Leonardus Lessius, S.J. (1554-1623).

Francis T. Hannafey, S.J., is Professor and Academic Advisor at
The Beijing Center for Chinese Studies. He has served for many
years as Associate Professor at Fairfield University, teaching
courses in Business Ethics and Contemporary Moral Problems.
He completed a Ph.D. in Ethics (1998) and an M.B.A. (1986)
at Loyola University Chicago. Professor Hannafey also holds
an M.Div. (1992) and S.T.M. (1993) from the Jesuit School at
Berkeley, California. Professor Hannafey's publications have
appeared in the Journal of Business Ethics, Business and Society
Review, Horizons, Louvain Studies, Theological Studies, The
Ecumenist, Spiritual Life, and elsewhere.

Simon G. M. Koo is the Executive Director of The Beijing Center.
He was a faculty member at the University of San Diego, UCSD,
and Santa Clara University. He was also the Associate Provost

of Jesuit Liberal Arts College in Hong Kong. A computer scientist and engineer by training, Dr. Koo's main research interest lies in the areas of network and data sciences, in which he led research projects and published over fifty reviewed articles as a scholar. Dr. Koo has taught a wide range of courses in Computer Science and Mathematics, as well as in Finance, Political Science, Architecture, and Chinese Philosophy. He received a Magoon Award for Excellence in Teaching, and was a recipient of the National Academy of Engineering CASEE New Faculty Fellowship in 2007. In addition, Dr. Koo is a serial entrepreneur, who founded multiple technology startups in Silicon Valley and Hong Kong. Dr. Koo is listed in *Who's who in America* and *Who's who of Emerging Leaders*, and he is a member of American Mensa.

Dr. Koo received his B.Eng. (Hons.) in Information Engineering with a minor in Mathematics from the Chinese University of Hong Kong, his M.S. in Electrical Engineering from NYU Tandon School of Engineering, his M.S. in Operations Research with emphasis on Financial Engineering from Columbia University, and his Ph.D. from the School of Electrical and Computer Engineering, Purdue University, West Lafayette. He is a senior member of IEEE and ACM, a member of Sigma Xi and Upsilon Pi Epsilon, and a fellow of the BCS.

Gianni Criveller, born in Treviso (Italy) has been based in Hong Kong and Greater China since 1991. Currently Criveller teaches Theology of Mission at the Holy Spirit Seminary College Philosophy and Theology in Hong Kong and Christology at the PIME International Theological Seminary in Monza (Milan). He has published about fifteen books and numerous essays in specialized journals (in various languages), and organized various international symposia. The Chinese translation of his first book, *Preaching Christ in Late Ming China* (Taipei-Brescia 1997) had two editions at the Sichuan People's Publishing House (Chengdu, China, 1999 and 2001). From 2010-2013, he was the head of the Historical Commission for the Beatification of Matteo Ricci, to whom Criveller has devoted many years of research and numerous writings.

About The Beijing Center

Established in 1998 by Ron Anton, S.J., The Beijing Center (TBC) is a not-for-profit center of higher education and research in mainland China committed to fostering mutual understanding between China and the rest of the world through cultural exchange, education, and research.

In its architecturally unique Beijing facility, TBC hosts students and scholars to study the Chinese language, culture, and all things China in China. Since 2002, TBC has partnered locally with the University of International Business and Economics (UIBE), a top-tier Chinese public research university. Throughout the years, over 2,000 students have spent a semester abroad at TBC and approximately 300–400 per year come to TBC with short-term faculty-led programs from North America, Latin America, Australasia, and Europe.

TBC maintains a research library with over 27,000 volumes in English, including rare books and maps, and hosts conferences, guest lectures, and seminars. Considered to be the largest English language library about China on the mainland, TBC has hosted numerous scholars from China and worldwide to assist with their research.

TBC serves as a hub for the international Jesuit higher education network in mainland China. What makes us unique is our place in a long and storied tradition, starting with Matteo Ricci, of Jesuit learning engaging with Chinese culture. This tradition teaches us that true cultural engagement starts with friendship.

Bibliography

Bernard, H. (1937). Le Père Matthieu Ricci et la société chinoise de son temps (1552-1610). In *Hautes études*.

Billings, T. (2009). *On Friendship: One Hundred Maxims for a Chinese Prince*. New York: Columbia University Press.

Brockey, L. M. (2009). *Journey to the East: The Jesuit Mission to China,1579-1724*. Cambridge: Harvard University Press.

Chinchilla, P. and A. Romano (Eds.) (2008). *La retórica de la imagen visual en la experiencia misional de la Compañía de Jesús en China (siglos XVII-XVJII): una evaluación a partir del estado de los estudios*. Mexico City: Universidad Iberoamericana.

Cicero (1923). Cato maior. In G. P. Goold (Ed.), *De Senectute*, London. Loeb Classical Library.

Corradini, P. (Ed.) (2000). *Della entrata della compagnia di Giesù e Christianità nella Cina*, Macerata. Quodlibet.

Corsi, E. (2012). Our little daily death Francesco Sambiasi's treatise on sleep and images in Chinese. In L. F. Barreto (Ed.), *Europe-China: Intercultural encounters (16th–18th centuries)*, Lisbon, pp. 79–96. Centro cientifico e cultural de Macao.

Criveller, G. (2009). The background of Matteo Ricci: The shaping of his intellectual and scientific endowment. In *Chinese Cross Currents*, Volume 6, pp. 72–93.

Criveller, G. (Ed.) (2011). *Matteo Ricci: Five Letters from China*, Beijing. The Beijing Center for Chinese Studies (TBC).

Criveller, G. (2014, May). The Dreams of the Melancholic Are True. Matteo Ricci's Ascent to Beijing. In *Beyond Thirty Nine. Hong Kong*. University of San Francisco.

D'Arelli, F. (Ed.) (1998a). *Dalla tradizione storiografica alle nuove ricerche'*. Rome: Istituto Italiano per l'Africa e l'Oriente.

D'Arelli, F. (1998b). Matteo Ricci e la traduzione latina dei quattro libri (sishu). dalla tradizione storiografica alle nuove ricerche. In *Le Marche e l'Oriente: Una tradizione ininterrotta da Matteo Ricci a Giuseppe Tucci*, pp. 163–175. Rome: Istituto Italiano per I' Africa e l'Oriente.

D'Arelli, F. (Ed.) (2001). *Ricci: Lettere (1580-1609)*, Macerata. Quodlibet.

del Gatto, M. (Ed.) (2000). *Della entrata della compagnia di Giesù e Christianita nella Cina*. Macerata: Quodlibet.

D'Elia, P. M. (Ed.) (1942). *Fonti Ricciane*, Volume I, Roma. Libreria dello Stato.

D'Elia, P. M. (Ed.) (1949a). *Fonti Ricciane*, Volume II, Roma. Libreria dello Stato.

D'Elia, P. M. (Ed.) (1949b). *Fonti Ricciane*, Volume III, Roma. Libreria dello Stato.

Dumortier, F. X. (2010). Introduction. In C. Shelke, M. Demichele, J. Vila-Chã, and E. Ryden (Eds.), *Matteo Ricci in Cina. Amicizia e fede (Matteo Ricci in China. Friendship and Faith): Inculturation through friendship and faith*, Rome. Gregorian Biblical Press.

Dunne, G. (1962). *Generation of Giants: The Story of the Jesuits in China in the last Decades of the Ming Dynasty*. Notre Dame, Indiana: University of Notre Dame Press.

Gernet, J. (1982). *China and the Christian Impact: A Conflict of Cultures*. Cambridge, U.K: Cambridge University Press.

Goodrich, C. and C. Fang (Eds.) (1976). *Dictionary of Ming Biography (1368-1644)*, New York. Columbia University Press.

Hsia, R. P.-C. (2010). *A Jesuit in the Forbidden City*. Oxford: Oxford University Press.

Hsia, R. P.-C. (2016). *Matteo Ricci & the Catholic Mission to China*. Indianapolis: Hackett.

Lancashire, D., K.-C. Hu, and E. Malatesta (1985). *The True Meaning of the Lord of Heaven* (Chinese-English ed.). St. Louis: Institute of Jesuit Sources.

Lancashire, D. and P. K.-C. HU (Eds.) (1985). *The True Meaning of the Lord of Heaven*, St. Louis. The Institute of Jesuit Sources.

Laven, M. (2011). *Mission to China: Matteo Ricci and the Jesuit Encounter with the East*. London: Faber and Faber Limited Bloomsbury House.

Levenson, J. R. (1964). *Confucian China and its Modern Fate*, Volume 3. Oakland, California: University of California Press.

Lin, J. (1987). Li madou jiaoyou renwubiao. In *Zhongwai Guanxishi Lucong*, Volume 1. Zhongguo Zhongwai Guanxishi Xuehui.

Luo, Y. (1986). *Li Madou Shuxinji*. Taipei: Kuangchi cultural Group and Fujen University Press.

Meynard, T. (2015). The first treatise on the soul in china and its sources an examination of the Spanish edition of the lingyan lishao by Duceux. In *Revista Filosófica de Coimbra*, Volume 47, pp. 203–242.

Pearman, W. D. (Ed.) (1883). *The dream of Scipio Africanus minor*, Cambridge. Deighton.

Pope Francis (2018, September). Message of His Holiness Pope Francis to the Catholics of China and to the Universal Church.

Reynolds, L. D. (Ed.) (1998). *De finibus bonorum et malorum*, Oxford. Clarendon Press.

Rienstra, M. H. (1986). *Jesuit Letters From China, 1583–1584*. Minneapolis: University of Minnesota Press.

Rule, P. A. (2010, May). What were "the directives of Matteo Ricci" regarding the Chinese rites? In *Pacific Rim Report*, Volume 54. University of San Francisco.

Seneca (1932). *De brevitate vitae*. London: William Heinemann.

Shelke, C. and M. Demichele (Eds.) (2010). *Matteo Ricci in China: Inculturation through Friendship and Faith*. Gregorian & Biblical Press.

Spence, J. (1980). *To Change China: Western Advisers in China, 1620–1960*. New York: Penguin Books.

Standaert, N. (1999). Jesuit corporate culture as shaped by the chinese. In *The Jesuits: Culture, Science and the Arts, 1540-1773*, Toronto. University of Toronto Press.

Standaert, N. (2010, May). Matteo Ricci: Shaped by the Chinese. In *Thinking Faith: The Online Journal of the British Jesuits*.

Vatican Information Service (2009, May). Matteo Ricci: A model of dialogue and respect for others.

Venturi, P. T. (Ed.) (1913). *Opere storiche del Padre Matteo Ricci, S.I.*, Macerata. Giorgetti.

Wicki, J. (Ed.) (1944). *Historia del principio y progresso de la Companía de Jesús en las Indias Orientales, 1542-1564 (History of the Commencement and Development of the Society of Jesus in the East Indies)*, Rome. Institutum Historicum S.I.

Xia, G. (Ed.) (1996). *Sheng Chao Po Xie Ji*, Hong Kong. Alliance Bible Seminary.

Yang, C. (1970). *Religion in Chinese Society: A Study of Contemporary Social Functions fo Religion and Some of their Historical Factors*. Berkeley: University of California Press.

Zheng, A. (Ed.) (2003). *Mingmoqingchu Yesuhui Sixiang Wenxian Huibian*, Beijing. Peking University Institute of Religion.

Zürcher, E. (2013). Xu guangqi and his anti-buddhism. In J. A. Silk and E. Zürcher (Eds.), *Buddhism in China: Collected Papers of Erik Zürcher*, Leiden, Boston, pp. 567–583. Brill.

30354337R00098

Made in the USA
San Bernardino, CA
24 March 2019